ENGLISH RECUSANT LITERATURE
1558–1640

Selected and Edited by
D. M. ROGERS

Volume 226

PETRUS FRARINUS
An Oration against the
Unlawfull Insurrections
1566

ST. COLETTE
The Declarations and Ordinances
Made upon the Rule
of . . . S. Clare
1622

PETRUS FRARINUS

An Oration against the
Unlawfull Insurrections
1566

The Scolar Press
1975

ISBN 0 85967 211 5

Published and printed in Great Britain by
The Scolar Press Limited, 59-61 East Parade,
Ilkley, Yorkshire and
39 Great Russell Street,
London WC1

NOTE

The following works are reproduced (original size), with permission:

1) Petrus Frarinus, *An oration*, 1566, from a copy in the Bodleian Library, by permission of the Curators.

References: Allison and Rogers 344; STC 11333.

2) St. Colette, *The declarations and ordinances*, 1622, from the unique copy in the library of Dún Mhuire, Killiney, Co. Dublin, by permission of the Librarian.

References: Allison and Rogers 245; not in STC.

AN ORATION

Against the Vnlawfull In-
surrections of the Protestantes of
our time, vnder pretence to
Reuourme Religion.
⁋Made and pronounced in Latin, in the
Schole of Artes at Louaine,
the. xiiij. of December.
Anno. 1565.
⁋By Peter Frarin of Andwerp, M. of
Arte, and Bacheler of both lawes.
And now translated into English,
with the aduise of the Authoz.

RESPICITE VOLATILIA COELI, ET PVLLOS CORVORVM

I F

ANTVERPIÆ,
Ex officina Ioannis Fouleri,
M. D. LXVI.

Epist.Iudæ.

Hi carnem quidē maculant , do-minationem autèm spernunt , maie-statem autèm blasphemant.

These, being deceiued by dreames, de-file the fleshe, despise the Rulers, & blas-pheme the Maiestie.

IBIDEM.

Hi sunt murmuratores querulosi, secundum desideria sua ambulantes.

These are murmurers, complainers, walking after their owne will.

IBIDEM.

Hi sunt qui segregāt semetipsos, animales, spiritum non habentes.

These are makers of sectes, fleshly, ha-uing no Spirite.

Prouerb.16.

Homo peruersus suscitat lites, & verbosus separat Principes.

A froward body causeth strife, & he that is full of words, maketh diuision among Princes.

A ij

The Extracte of the Priuilege.

Catholicæ Maiestatis speciali gratia permissum est Petro Frarino Antuerpiensi, vt per quem seu quos voluerit Typographorum admissorum impunè ei liceat imprimi curare et per omnes has suæ Ditionis regiones distrahere Orationem Anglicè inscriptam: An Oration against the vnlawfull Insurrections of the Protestantes: Eiusdemq; Maiestatis Priuilegio cautum expressè, ne quisquàm eandem Orationem proximis quinquè annis absq; predicti Petri consensu imprimat vel alibi impressam distrahat. Si quis contra hác Regiam prohibitionem ausu temerario committere vel ei fraudem facere attentauerit, sciat se non futurum immunem à pœna contenta in diplomate dato in Regiæ Maiestatis Concilio priuato Bruxellæ 14. Martij. Anno. 1565. stilo Brabantiæ.

Subsig.

Bourgeois.

The Translatour to the Gentle Reader.

AMong many other laudable cuſtomes of ỹ noble Vniuerſitie of Louaine, this one is yearely obſerued there, that in ỹ moneth of December al ordinarie leſſons ceaſe for the ſpace of one whole weeke, and in place thereof ſome Learned man is choſen by common aſſent to be the Preſident of certaine Diſputations: wherein he proponeth, to ſuch as are thereto appointed, diuerſe frutefull queſtions in Diuinitie, Law, Phyſik Phyloſophie, Humanitie, and in all probable matters, making argumentes breefly for both partes of ỹ queſtions, and then leauing to ỹ iudgemẽt

A iij ofthe

of the *Respondent* to chuse whiche parte he liketh beste (whereof those exercises haue theyr name) and the next daye folowing in that place to handle the same *Rhetoricallie* the space of two houres together wout interruption, in presence and hering of the whole *Vniuersitie* there then assembled. And in this maner twise a day fower houres are spente that weeke, with greate profite and vtterance of many good and profitable maters of learning worth the hering and bering away, though litle thereof commonly afterward come forth in printe, to the sight and vewe of the world.

Amonge diuerse other, this laste December there, a learned man toward the *Law* called M. *Peter Frarin*

Disputationes Quodlibeticæ.

rin borne in Andwerp made an Oration against the Insurrections of the
Protestantes and Sectes of our time,
not without greate commendation,
which, at the earnest requeste of his
frindes, he suffered to be afterwarde
printed. Anh because I thought it no
lesse profitable and fruteful, that, as
that Oration is in Latine, and like to
be shortly in Doutch and Frenche,
so it should be in Englishe also to
warne my deere Contremen of those
mens malice and cruelty: I conferred
with him, and by his aduise traslated
it into our Mother tong, with suche
notes and farther additiõs as for lack
of tyme, whē he pronounced it, werē
omitted and leafte out in the Latine.
VVherein I toke such leaue and ly-
bertie, as the Author, with whome I

conferred, might be bolde to vſe him
ſelfe in his owne doinges, or geue an
other man, and as the Vayne of our
Engliſſhe tong ſeemed beſte to beare
in ſuch kind of talke, leauing ſometymes the preciſe wordes of ẙ Latin,
but neuer ſwaruing any whit from
the truthe. And for the aſſurance
and prouſe of ẙ matter of this whole
Treatiſe, the Author proteſteth that
he vttered nothing in all this oration
againſte any man, but that either he
ſawe with his owne eyes, or harde of
credible perſons that were preſent
at thoſe maters, or read in approued
VVriters, or in theyr owne bookes
whom he chargeth, or finally that is
notoriouſly knowen to whole Cities
and Countries.

Take therefore, I beſeeche thee
Gentill

Gentill Reader, in good parte this faire warning thou haste here to take heede of these perilouse pretended Reformers. and weighe rather the mater, then my rude vtterance in Englisshe. And if thou be a Gentelman, learne here what these miens intent and practise is againste all noble Stockes. They meane vtterlie to roote out ỹ Nobilitie and al noble Bloud, as they haue done alreadie at Geneua, and in those Cátons of Suitzerland, where this fifte Gospell reigneth. The deputies that represented the three estates of Burgundie in their Discourse vppon the Frenche Kings Edicte of pacification are my Authors of this reporte. If thou be a Ruler and in authority, con-

Remonstrances au Roy des depu tes des trois e-stats de Burgoigne iur l' edict de la pacification: part.2.

confyder their confpiracies and trea-
fons againft all Magiftrates. If thou
be a mā of the Churche, marke here
their malice and extreme crueltie
against all Gods true Minifters and
Vertuous Priefts. If thou be a faithfull fubiecte amonge the Commons,
fee theyr robberies; theyr pouling
and rifling, theyr vnmercifull ex-
torfions, theyr vnfatiable greadines
in gatheringe to them other mens
goodes. Finallie, if thou be a true
Chriftian man, Abhorre and detefte
theyr VVickednefse, Sacrilege,
horrible blafphemies, and impietie againft God and all his holy Myf-
teries. To be fhort, I trufte no man
wilbe offended with the reading of
thisOration, but only fuch as in their

owne

owne consciences feele them selues
guyltie of these cõspiracies and treasons herein mentioned, and therfore
seeme to be touched nere the quicke.
And yet perhappes, by Gods grace,
this soure medicine, though it smart,
may worke in some of them also, first
shame, then repentance, and last a-
mendement of suche vngodly pourposes and enterprises, and call them
backe againe thither, wherehence
they fell, to doe their former workes,
as the Spirit of trueth sayeth, in the Apoca.2.
fear of God, the vnity of his Church,
obedience of theyr Princes, and charitie with theyr neighbours. But
sure I am, it will litle please M. Ie-
wel and his Companiõs, who by wryting, preaching and printing, First
prouoked with great confidence and
bragges

brags the Catholikes to wryte their
mindes in matters of controuersie
and queſtions about Religion, wiſ-
ſhing that the Queenes grace, (for
whome we daily pray) woulde not
onlye licenſe them, but commaunde
them to wryte: And now that diuers
haue wrytten full learnedly to their
confuſion and ſhame (meddling nothing with the affaires and politike
Gouernment of the Realme, but only with poyntes of Doctrine) they
haue none other way to anſwere and
make their party good, but to turne
their tale, chainge their tune, and
report that the wrytinges of the Catholikes are ſeditious, and tende to
the diſquieting and diſturbaunce of
the Commonweale, that the authors
thereof are vnnaturall and diſorde-
red

red *subiectes* : and so by *suche false informations* labour to procure the meanes to *stay* and let to come into the *Realme suche Bookes* as *detecte* their *Vntruthe, Falshode,* and *Herefies,* and are most profitable for all good *Christians* and true *Subiectes* to reade, in these daungerous daies.

If they *practise* the like *againste* this little *discourse* made *againste Commotions* for *Religion,* they shall declare plainly and make the worlde understande, that they are not true *Subiects* to the *Queenes Maiestie,* nor yet faithfull to the *Nobilitie,* nor frindefull to the *Commons* of their owne natiue *Countrie.* For here is nothing but a *Detection* of false and wicked *Treasons againste Princes* and *Rulers,* and, as it were, a hole=

some

To the Reader.

some Triacle for Magistrates and
faithfull Subiectes, against the con-
tagious infection and daugerous pe-
stilence of rebellion. Fare well Gen-
tle reader , and with the manners
and behauioure thou seest in our Mi-
nisters at home compare and laye to-
gether these Straunge doinges of
their Fellowes and Companions a-
brode in other Countries. So shalt-
thou perceiue, they are of one sprite
Math.7. *and stampe , and (according to the*
Counsell of Christ the sonne of God)
know them by their workes, as y tree
is knowen by his frute , and by that
meanes learne to auoid them, and
beware of them. From And-
werp. Maij. 9. Anno.
1566.

Ihon Foules.

Againste the vnlawfull
insurrections of the Pro-
testantes of our time, vnder
pretése to refourme Religion.

Two principall thinges in euerie Cōmon weale haue at all tymes bene especially esteemed and taken for the chief. both which now in this our age throughout al Christendom the desperat boldnes of certaine most wicked persons hath disturbed : I meane, Religion, and Peace.

The question of God allmightie his true Religiō prophaned, I leaue to those men to handle, to whose custodie and credite the holy Mysteries of Christian Religion are, by the diuine Authoritie of Gods ordinance, committed: whose learning, wit, and eloquence may further muche the defense of so weighty a mater, whose Profession, Authoritie and vertue,
ought

ought to be alwaies emploied about ſuch Godlie affaires.

The other argument, that is, of Peace broken by Seditions, of Publike and good Order troubled, of Magiſtrates, vnder pretenſe of reformation, contemned, of God and mans law offended and tranſgreſſed, ꝩ cauſe and lamētable matter I had alſo at this time gladly omitted, leauing it to the handling of the eloquente and wiſe, that are practyſed in Publike affaires, grounded in knowlege of the lawes, and weightie Policies of Princes: had it not bene, that I was at this preſent firſt moued to take the rueful Diſcours thereof in hand by the earneſt requeſt of ſuch, to whome lightelie, without inſt excuſe, I may deny nothing: then, lead (as it were) thereto by hope and regard of your moſt courteouſe gentelnes and patience (right worſhipfull Audience) and finally drawen and driuen to ſpeake by force of the hatred I bare to ſo vile and villanouſe a mater, leaſt, perhaps as by mine, ſo by all other mens ſilence ſo hainouſe a thing ſhould haue eſcaped quite vnſpoken of.

FOr

For in very deed when I considered & weighed the matter w̃ my self, mine opinion told me thus, That this right worthy Seat wherin I now stand, was not alwaies to be the place ope only to most eloquent Oratours, occupied most commõlie by most graue and auncient Doctors, whose accustomed maner hath bene to bring hither, and to poure into your most learned eares nothing but such stuf as was inuented by great wit, framed w̃ much diligence, atcheiued & finished with grauitie, iudgement, arte and eloquence. And as for me, were it so ỹ I had al other thinges requisite to such a one that worthely might attempt this publike exercise and entrie of cõmendation in matters of learning: yet (to saie the verie truthe) I thought myne age scarse ripe enough for the graue rome of this so worshipfull a Place. And withal, besides these defectes, this also did put me in verie great feare, least as somtymes Demosthenes, ỹ cheife Pere of al Greke eloquēce, framing hym self to speake in ỹ presence of Philip king of the Macedons, happened in the very beginning of his Oration to stay, to lack

B   vtte-

vtterance & wordes, being astonied with the Royall Maiesty of so great a personage: so in like sort I, addressing my selfe to talke in this so great an asséble of most learned Audiéce, shuld haue peradnéture the very same, or y̆ like chaúce & fortune.

But this needelesse donbt, and feare, proceding of the fainte & bashfull shamefastnesse of youth, was at length somewhat dissolued by the comfortable exhortations of my frendes, and is now at last quite remoued and put away by the most chearefull sight of this your gentle presence and pleasant countenances, wherewith I fele sensibly my self to be maruelously now refreshed & pronoked, as it were, to speake boldly & with good courage. For who wold be afraid to speak of Seditions in the presence of suche quiet persons? Against treasons, before moste faithful Subiects? who would doubt in the hearing of Officers and Magistrates, to talke against tumultes, robbing, stealing, cóspiracies, cutting of throtes, spoiling of Countreis, burning of Cities, sacking of Churches, wicked sacrilege,& most impiouse contempt of thinges apper pertaining to God, & finally againſt the very bane and peſtilence of all commendable alliaunce and vnitie of Common weales, & the vtter ruine and deſtruction of all Ciuill Policy and good Order: For what one man of you all (right honorable & worſhipfull) wold gladly or willingly allow and beare ſuche & ſo hainous enormities in any Realme or Conntry?

I wil therfore go forward in my matter & ſpeake: yea, & now hauing gathered courage by y aſſured hope of your gentle patience, I wil ſay boldly, that the Proteſtantes of our time haue not done well in putting them ſelues in armes vnder colour of refourming Religion : y they haue done therein againſt all law, right and equitie , not without intolerable iniury, damage and wrong in euery reſpect to y Publike eſtate of Chriſtendome. In this poynt conſiſteth y whole weight and controuerſy of the queſtion y was yeſterday (according to the cuſtome of this ſchole) proponed to be the argumēt of my talke at this time.

I will firſt open and declare vnto you, y there was no cauſe or iuſt occaſion, why theſe men ſhuld riſe & make inſurrection.

2 Then, that they toke weapon in hand without any authozity, cõtrary to law, & in deſpite of al Magiſtrates and Rulers.

3 Laſt and finallie, ỹ they vſed thẽſelues to cruelly, & handled their ſwerd to blou-dily, to the greateſt damage, hyndzance & loſſe, that euer was felt in Chziſtendome.

With theſe limites and boundes I make, as it were, a trauerſe and cloſe my ſelf within a circle, out of the cumpaſſe whereof the diſcourſe and ozder of my talke ſhall not ſtraie: that by theſe mea-nes both I, out of infinite matter that offreth it ſelf in the hãdling of this cauſe, may haue certen ſpecial pointes marked and choſen wherof I may treat, and alſo you, euen now before hand, may fozſee & beare in mynd, in hearing what things, your learned eares are lyke to be em-ploied during myne Ozation.

I deny vtterlie, ỹ there was any good oz reaſonable cauſe, whie the founders & bzokers of this new Goſpel ſhuld be dzi-nen oz pzouoked to put them ſelues in armes againſt the Catholikes. This is ỹ firſt poynt wherof I pzomiſed to ſpeake.

whiles

whiles in few wordes J declare & proue this vnto you, J humblie request you, to diligent attention to mark and geue eae.

Jt behoueth alwayes, ꝑ there be very great causes proued why, before chainge of lawes ſhuld be in any common weale procured: & in very deed it ought to be a marueloulse occaſion & the greateſt cauſe of all cauſes, whē the innouation of Religion (being alway ꝑ very backebone of al realmes both Chriſtian and Heathen) ſhuld be attempted. But that either this or that ſhould be don by force and armes, by warre & rebellion, by fier & ſwerd, by murder and bloudſhed of the good and faithfull Subiectes, there can neuer any reaſon or ſufficiente cauſe be alleged or brought why and wherefore.

J remēber, amōg many other notable lawes, wherwith in times paſt the Locreñſes ruled their cōmon weale, it was with great policy and wiſdom ordained, ꝑ if any mā wold go about to procure anī chainge in the publike aſſaires of ꝑ eſtate, he ſhuld ſtand vp in a high place, & there hence ſpeake his minde freely to the people, being then there aſſēbled about him:

but yet with this condition, that all the while he ſpake, he ſhould haue a rope tied with a riding knot looſe inough about his necke, the which rope ſhould be ſo lõg, that the other end therof might lie on the ground betwene their feete that hard his diſcourſe & deuiſe: to this effect, that, if in ẙ end of his tale ẙ people wer perſwaded that it was for their cõmon cõmodity and profit, to make that chainge and innouation as he had ſaid, then he ſhoulde come downe without any harme, and be dimiſſed with muche commendation and fauor: els the Audience out of hãd might pull the rope and reuenge with preſent death the raſh attempt and ſeditious enterpriſe of ſuch a one as wythout good cauſe, beſtowed his buſy braine about chainges and alterations.

If it had pleaſed the Princes and Rulers of ẙ world in this our time to haue eſtabliſhed and practiſed this lawe, we ſhould haue no nede now to ſighe at the ſight of ſo miſerable a confuſion, diſorder and troublous ruffling of all things. we ſhould not haue ſene of late, and yet ſee this ſo lamêtable an eſtate of the world,

ſo

so many warres, Tumultes, Slaughters, Ruines, so many Churches suppressed, so many Townes ouerturned. finally we should not now rue so many wicked Sacrileges comitted in prophaning of Gods Mysteries, & sacred things appertaining to his Honor and Seruice.

But alas it was free, without any feare of the rope for these authors and fosterers of Sectes, frankly and boldly to perswade with the people, and bestowe their wordes as they liste. And would God they had staied there, and had disbursed nothing but vernished woordes: they wente further from woordes to woundes and Blowes. They hadde the word in their mouthes, the Sword in their handes: their word sounded peace, theyr Sword coyned war: their peace serued for a guylful cloke to couer crafte and deceyt, their war was employed to execute violence, crueltie and murder. was there none other meanes to plant that bloddy Gospell, but to attempt Reformatió in ý state of ý Churche by ciuil warres, insurrections and Rebellion? Put vp thy sword in the sheth,

B iiij   saied

ſaied Chriſt to S. Peter: Oute with thy
ſword for the Goſpell, ſayeth the new
Goſpeller. There was a Companie of
deſperat & wicked perſonnes ẏ ran lyke
mad men vp and down the ſtreates of
Paris with gliſtering naked ſwordes in
theyr handes, and cried out, the Gospel,
the Goſpell: when they meant nothing
els, but to bring a ſort of curſed Sectes
and wicked Hereſies into the Realme.

It was not (I aſſure you honorable &
worſhipfull) it was not the Goſpel they
brought, except they hold it for a Goſpel to cut in pieces, to ſacke, ſpoile and
quite to ouerthrow wᵗ blowes & naked
ſword all ẏ ẏ Euangeliſtes buylded wᵗ ẏ
word. It was not Gods quarell at all:
that bloudy bickering was neuer taken
in hand for Gods ſake. And in this be-
half I call to wittnes euen the ſelf ſame
man, that was our moſt earneſt & fierce
aduerſarie in this queſtion, who was ẏ
occaſion of al our calamitie, and was the
Author and maker of this lamentable
Tragedie. In this matter, I ſay, I call
thee, frier Luther to witnes. For out of
whoſe mouth (I pray thee) fell ẏ worthie
saying

Claud.
de Sain-
ctes du
Saccage-
ment
des egli-
ſes. fol.
57.

saieng in the noble assemble of ẏ learned
and honorable at Lipsia: Neither was this
matter euer begonne for Gods quarell,
nother shalbe ended for Gods sake. O
noble sentence, and worthie in deed to
come out of his mouth, that would be
called ẏ heauenly Prophete, ẏ third Elias, ẏ fifth Euāgeliste. was this matter,
say you, neuer begonne for Gods sake?
I beleue it wel. what was then ẏ cause,
I pray you good syr, ẏ ye made so cruel,
so long, so deadlie warre against ẏ Christians, ẏ ye sticked not to trouble al Chri
stendome wt ciuil batayle, wt insurrectiōs
& vproies, wt tumultes, seditiō, & rebellion? ẏ ye could find in yout hartes, to
fight against your own parētes, & your
own childrē, against your Rulers & magistrates, yea & against ẏ church of christ?

war ought neuer to be made without
most waighty occasion. For it is ẏ part of
a wise mā to try all meanes & waies, rather thē to lay hād on his weapon: but ẏ
mē shuld fight at home in their own coū-
trie against their own felows, their own
neighbors, their own parēts, there is no
reson nor cause ẏ euer cā be foūd for it: or
surely

Luth. in
disput.
Lipsic.
1519.
teit. D.
Empier.
D. Eck.
& Legat.
tum ibi
præsī.

surely if any be, it is this, that it be don by Cōmission & lawful authority for Gods honor, for Gods sake only, & for none other respect: & you, sir Luther, do flatly, (and yet most truly) deny, that these your doinges were for any suche reipect at all.

If I were able to say nothing in this matter, but this ỹ thou thy self saiest for me, yet out of doubt, by ỹ verdict & iugemēt of al honest, wise, & indiscrēt men, I should preuail in this cause, and proue al your sect to be seditious, rash, cruel, wicked, traiterous against God & man, for ỹ without any iust occasiō, ye haue so long & so cruelly troubled the whole estate of Christendō. But you say, ỹ faith was wel nigh quite quēched, & out of the Church. It is a wonderous matter ye speake of. Christ praied for S. Peter, that his Faith shuld neuer faile. And wil ye say, he praid in vaine, lost his labor, and could not obtain his prayer? that were iniury and reproche to the sonne of God. The holye Ghost came downe from heauen into the Church here militant on earth, to teache her al truth. Hath he not taught her? you blaspheme the holy Ghost, so to say.

But

But goe to: let it be graunted that, as you imagine all maner of fonde & absurd thinges, so you thought in this poynte with no lesse madnesse, that the Christian Faith was lost, or at least that Christian Religion being nigh outworne and spēt before your happy daies needed to be restored by such excellent, graue, godly, and wise men as you were, replenished with all maner of knowledge, vertue and heauenly giftes of the sprite.

To be short, your purpose was, ye say, to refourme the Christian Faith. Howe then? when you could not therin preuail, nor perswade the people, that was somewhat stubburn and stiffeneckcd perhaps as you iudged, did you thinke it the best way by and by with gonneshot, and byrels to beat and driue the faith into their heades?

who euer being in his right wit did thinke, that any thing might be perswaded by force? Men vse to perswade the minde and not the bodye: but it is moste certaine, that the minde, as it maye be bent, led, and induced by reason, so by stripes, blowes & buffets it can neuer be

com-

compelled and conſtrained. But it was a carnal Religion ẏ theſe fleſhly Goſpellers brought and taught, & therefore they dyd what they could to driue it into mens braynes with ſtrokes, and to prick it into mens fleſh with ſwordes, dags, and daggers. It may be, ye were muche offended wͭ the vitiouſe maners and ill liuing of men now a dayes. In good faith and ſo were we. there is no honeſt Catholike man that euer was delighted therwith. But yet when we ſaw that it was very hard fully to cleanſe & purge anie one familie or howſhold frō all maner of ſynnes & ſores, we thought it a matter of far greater difficultie & importance, to amend the faultes & heale ẏ wondes of al the whole corps of Chriſtēdom together. therfore of neceſſity, becauſe we could not remedie ẏ deſperate caſe by reaſon of the multitnde, we bore wͭ ẏ cōmon and vulgare Deceaſes and vices of al ſortes of men, the cure wherof was more paſt hope, and did take them patientlye, but yet ſurely not without great greif and ſorow to ſee them & open preaching cōtinuallie againſt them. But
yon

you (sowz Checkmasters & most bitter Controllers of maners) went about, lyke Judges sent from heauen oz Physitions dzopte owt of the skyes, to cōdēne and cut of with swozd, & burn with fire and gunpowder all at a pushe y faultes and folies of the whole wozld together.

Yf ye had bene officers hauing Commissiō and authoritie so to doe, yet your Judgement and pzocesse could not be excused herein from exceding crueltie and raishnes: but where it appeareth ye were but slingbzaynes & light Jackstrawes hauing no authozitie at al, y toke vppō you, without any examinatiō, without pzocesse of law, without any sentence, to condemne al Chzistendome, to rack it, to punish it, and with most greuouse and painefull tozmentes to teare and turne vpsyde down y whole wozld: what shall I call this but a bloudy Butcherie, a haynous wickednes, a dyuelish dealing, an inpietie neuer to be pardoned? O but (say you) the Catholikes did lyue vitiously, the Cleargie were out of ozder, the Pzinces and Rulers ruled not as they should: yea & there were manie ceremonies in y Churche y we could not bzook.

I assure you these be greuous & weighty Inditementes. who laid them in, I pray you? who but you, the worst men, & naughtiest liuers ý euer trode on earth? What blames the theese Verres his mate? Or cutthrote falles with Myles at bate.

The third Elias him self did playnlye confesse, that the manners of men were far more vitious vnder his Gospel, then euer they wer before vnder ý Popedome. He hath said it. It is not lawful to gainsay ý same. But if any of ý disciples dare deny that, which this theyr great master Pythagoras sayde, the beddes are yet warme wherin these gospellers lay with other mennes wiues: the Townes and Cities smoke yet of the fire, wherewith they burned houses: the earth is moiste at this houre with the bloude of manye good subiectes whome they haue slaine: theyr Purses do swel, and are yet at this present puft vp with the goods they gathered, and gaines they got by roberies, Simonye, and Extortion.

Shew forthe thy brasen face, Martin Luther, and saye if thou dare, that thou art an honester and better man, then the

very

Marginal notes:

Quid fur accusat Verrem, homicida Milonem?

Georg. Wicel. in retect. Luth. & Luth. in sua postilla su. Dō: 1. aduētus.

vertuous and graue Fathers and Pre=
lates of the Catholike Churche: I wyll
out of hād bring in against thee, the pub=
like Edict that the most noble Charles
the fift our late soueraigne Emperour of
happy memory, made againste thee at
wormes: the witnesse of the greate and
mightye Henry the eight King of Eng=
land, whose sacred Royall crowne (be it
spoken here with leaue) thou, like a slut=
tish slaue, vauntest, thou wouldst anoynt
with durt and donge of thy dronken bo=
dy: The decree of the most renoumed Si=
gismund king of Pole: and by these eui=
dences I wil by and by conuince thee, &
proue that thou art worthy to be caste, of
Rebellion, Sedition, Sacrilege, Impie=
ty, Heresy: Finally of all manner of wic=
ked vices and hainous offences that can
raigne in a man. what canst thou lay a=
gainst these witnesses, who were, at that
time, the noblest, the best, the worthiest of
credite, of all that liued in our daies?

Theese worthy Princes Proclamati=
ons and Publike Edictes sette oute a=
gainste thy wickednesse and Naughtye
beha=

(marginal notes:) Edict Worm. Carol. 5. contr. Luth. An. 1521. Resp. Regis Ang. ad ep. Lut. ep. ad Duces Saxon. Lut. li cont R Angl. Edict. Re. Polo con. Lutheranos

behauioure, are euery where in euery mans hande published in print to the vewe and sight of the whole world.

Come vp againe hither frō hell, if thou canst Jhon Caluine, & tel truth seing al ẏ world knoweth, ẏ thou diddest kepe ẏ space of fiue yeares together a Nunne, who was a Renegate out of ẏ Nūnerie called Weilmur: ẏ thou diddest paye two crownes a moneth for her borde in the towne out of ẏ poore mens boxe of Geneua, vppon condition she should come euery day to make thy bedde and learne her lesson out of thy Gospell, & practize how to beare ẏ burden of wedlocke patiently: and at last, when she was great wͦ childe by thee, and had now caried abowt ẏ burden of her bealie three or fower monethes, that thou didst bestow vppon an Apostate Chanon dwelling at Losanna thereby, both the cow and the calf in mariage, a Gods name, as thou calleste it, but honest mē were euer wont to call it sacrilegiouse whoordome.

Denie, if thou dare, Theodore Beza, ẏ, according to ẏ Gospell of thy Apostle & master Simō Magus, thou diddest sell twise to two diuers mē for readie monie

This is written in a frenche boke intitled Passauant Parisien printed at Paris in S. James streat at the signe of the Elephāt. ꝛ.1559.

See the preface of Beza his confessiō.

thy ſpiritual liuinges, whereof thou haddeſte in Fraunce many moꝛe then thou
were woꝛthy of, foꝛ the which thy lewd
and duble dealing the byers that bought
thy benefices, hauing now by the lawe
loſt them, pꝛocured thee to be denoũced
excommunicate, and to be pꝛoclaimed foꝛ
a notoꝛiouſe Excommunicate perſon by
the Crier, about all the market places of
Paris: Denie, if thou canſte foꝛ ſhame,
that now at this pꝛeſent in Loſanna thou
keepeſt, vnder the falſe name of pꝛe-
tenſed mariage, in filthie adulterie, the
wife of a pooꝛe Tayloꝛ, who, excepte he
be lately dead, dwelleth yet in the Har-
peſtreate at Paris: That when ſhe (her ᴹiſtreſſe
name, as thou calleſte her, is Miſtres beautis.
Candida) fledde to Dewlo the common
Stewes at Paris from her houſt ande
(becauſe, hauing taken her in adulterie
he had geuen her a gaſhe with a knyfe
in the hip, and becauſe ſhe had bene put
in priſon, foꝛ that ſhe ſet hte a friſcoll,
when ſhe was merily dawn ing in a
wine tauerne w her cuſtomers, and ſayd,
hoighe one leape moꝛe foꝛ all Chriſten
ſoules) thou cammeſt thither to riſpe

L j   and

and comfort her, and to currie fauor, and when thou haddeſte made a filthie boke of vile and bawdie verſes and rimes in her prayſe, at length thou tokeſte her away therehence, and hauinge made a greate purſe of mony, by Simonie, Sacrilege and ſpoilinge of Churches, thou cariedſt her away with thee to Geneua, where Caluine ſollennized a mariage betwen you. As for thy other moſt wicked doeinges afterward in Fraunce I ſay nothinge at this tyme.

what ſhal I here rekon vp and open to your learned cares ye vile behauiour, the leacherous liuing, the abhominable adulteries, the filthie whoordomes, the dubblenes, the robberies, the crueltie, the Sacriledges, of other of the ſame ſtampe, who vnder colour of Religion and hypocritical name and Title of Miniſters and Goſpellers deceaue and beguyle the whole worlde? To make few wordes, the abiects & outcaſtes, the moſt wicked and baſe of all ſortes of men are gon to this goſpellyſh Cõgregation like chaf winowed out of Gods floore, or like as vile ſilth & ordure doth run & flow in
to a

to a ſtinking gutter oʒ ſinke. But eſpe=
cially if we cõſider ẙ Patriarches of this
Synagog, the chief Authoʒs, the makers
and Maſters of theſe Sectes: we ſhall
plainly ſee, as in part I haue declared of
the thʒefoʒenamed Captains, ẙ ther was
neuer in the Church of Chʒiſt ſuch wedes
ſpʒong vp, ſo lewd, ſo lecherous, ſo
pʒoud, ſo arrogant, ſo ſpitefull, ſo mali=
riouſe, ſo wicked. Foʒ they are ſo clad
with al manner of naughtines, that ther
is noʒ hand, noʒ foote voied of vice, noʒ
any one part of all theyʒ bodies vnſpot=
ted, noʒ any wicked acte abſent from
theyʒ whole ſynfull carcaſſes.

O ẙe vertuous Reſourmoʒs, could ye
beare with all theſe abhominations in
your owne manners, & could abyde no=
thing amiſſe among Catholike mẽ? The
flame of your fyʒie Charitie was ſo hot,
that ye dydde your beſte to burne vp
quite other mens faultes, yea, the men
themſelues, theyʒ Cities, houſes, dwel=
linges and all. But ye would not ſo
muche as ſweale your owne Coates
with the leaſte ſparkle of that conſu=
minge fyʒe.

E ij If

If all they that had offended moſt, had firſt ſuffered puniſhemēt proportionable to their deſertes, you had gon to the pot ere this: it had bene your lot, who euery one of you haue moſte wickedly tranſgreſſed God and mans law, to haue gon firſt to the gallowes. Would God that order of inſtice had bene obſerued: there had bene by this tyme not one of that your wicked packe and Conſpiracie lefte aliue to puniſh the Catholikes ſo cruelly with warre, fire, and ſword, liued they wel or yll.

But you can ſpare your ſelues well inough, & are in ẏ meane time ſo ſtreight laced, that ye cannot find in your cankered conſciences to pardon any offenſe in other men. Ye were ſo inflamed with the zeale of the Goſpell and of Godes houſe, that ye cried out againſt the Catholikes and proclaimed them Superſtitiouſe, Adulterers, Tirannes, Idolatres &c. If all be true, as you ſay, in deed it is a weightie mater worthie to be ſharpely loked vpon that ye lay in againſt them. But if all theſe be but lyes, fables, and falſe ſurmiſes of your owne mali-

malitioufe ſtomakes, as they be in dede, then you vncharitable backbiters, you moſt impudent ſclaunderers, haue deſerued to abide your ſelues the inſt puniſhmēt due to thoſe faultes, ye falſly fathered vpon other. But ye were wily foxes, ye eſcaped well enough. For ye did not, I warāt you, as ẏ law ordaineth, put your names to the inditemētes ⟨& accuſations ſubſcribed with your owne handes to bind your ſelues to be readie to receaue the puniſhement of the faultes ye layed againſt other, if ye failed in your proofs. Yea, and ye behaued yourſelues yet more impudently thē this, and more contrary to all order, proceſſe, and forme of lawful proceding : for in this your monſtrous iudgement of Reformation, you wer the accuſers your ſelues, and you, the ſelfe ſame men, the witneſſes, the iudges, the hangmen, and moſt cruell boutchers to execute your owne vnlawfull ⟨& wicked ſentence. It may be, this touched you neere ẏ quick and cauſed you to winche and ſtrike, that becauſe of your profeſſion and vow of perpetual chaſtitie, wherein ye promiſed to liue chaſte during your

Pœna Talionis

Subſcrip tio in crimen.

lines, ye were not ſuffred freely to mary, to beguile pooꝛe ſimple women, to bathe your filthy bodies in the ſtinking puddle of carnall pleaſures. what then? It had bene your parte to ſtande to your owne pꝛomiſe, though ye had made it to your moꝛtall enemie: howe muche moꝛe had it becomme you, to haue kepte the vowe of Chaſtitie ye made to God almightie? But twyſſhe: you were werie of your vowe, it repented you that euer you made it, ye dyd ſette naught by it, ye were of that mynde peraduenture, that ye had rather be damned foꝛ euer, then to treade foꝛ a ſhoꝛte ſpace the ſtreight narowe way that leadeth to heauen.

Wel, if it were ſo that nedes ye would to it, and caſte your Vowe on the hedge: yea needed not ſtreight wayes to fight foꝛ the mater. Foꝛ ye had the common Stewes and bꝛothell houſes open at all tymes, and euery where at your plea= ſure. Lighte women maried, and vn= maried, yea and Nunnes that had pꝛo= feſſed Virginitie, as you had done, were ready by your lewd perſwaſions (moꝛe was the pittie) to ſerue your filthye luſtes,

Fides hoſti ſer- uanda.

luſtes, to keepe you companie, to goe
to the diuell arme in arme with you.

But what if perhappes ſome of you
dwelled among good men in ſuche well
ordered Townes, where good Rule
was ſo narowly loked to, that by no
meanes they could be ſuffred to haue a
Miſtreſſe Candida for a veſſell of eaſe‑
ment, as ye call it: was that a ſufficient
wrong and iuſte quarell for you to take
Pepper in the noſe, and ſworde in the
hande, and by and by bidde Battaile?
were ye bound to ſtand ſo ſtoutly to La‑
die Lecherie, Dame Venus, to maintain
the liberties of her Kingdome and Goſ‑
pel ſo ſtreightly, that if euery one of you
in euery place were not permitted free‑
ly and without checke to cheriſhe his
carkaſſe with a whore, ye ſhoulde for re‑
uenge of her quarell trouble the Goſ‑
pell of Chriſte, diuide with Sciſmes
the Churche of God, make ſuche a ſee‑
dition, ſuche a ſturre, ſuche an vproze in
all Chriſtendome, as neuer any Bar‑
barons, Rude, Sauage or wild people
made the like?

Some of your ſide ſuffred for ſ words
C iiŋ ſake

It is Co‑
uerdales
Phraſe.

ſake, for ſo ye cal ẏ curſed goſpel of yours
Yea and well worthy to , I aſſure you.
For they neuer ceaſed to bark at Prelats
& Princes, to worke al meanes to wring
the ſword out of theyr handes, to trouble
and diſorder ẏ ſtate of common weales:
Finally they neuer had theyr ful of theyr
ſundrie wicked practiſes againſt God,
of theyr raiſhe madneſſe and furiouſe
blaſphemies againſt the bleſſed Sacrament of the Altar.

Yea, but you ſaie it was the very true
worde of God they preached , they were
the men of God, the Martyrs of Ieſus
Chriſt, the Apoſtels of Chriſtendome.
Theſe be high Titles . will they be any
higher? I wil ſpeake for them, to ſet thē
vp one ſteppe more . They were thoſe
that labored to clyme vp to the North, to
place theyr ſeates aboue ẏ cloudes of the
heauens, to be like Lucifer, Checkmates
with God himſelf. And what of al thie?
was it meete that becauſe they could not
freely and frankely preache the worde,
therefore by and by they ſhould lay hand
on the ſword?

I ẏ

The Apostles of Jesus Christe were wōt to suffer, not to gene blowes: to take not to doe iniury. S. Paule was cōtent rather to leese his head, and paciently to suffer the sword, then to strike or cause any to reuenge his quarell . S. Peter was wrongfully crucified, and yet procured no man to be troubled for it. why do not the new Apostles folow the olde Apostles example?

O Master Ministers, it is a very hard word ÿ ye bring vs. for ye speake gōnestones, your Gospel is to hot, ye preache fire and powder , your Religion is to cruell, it breedeth bloud and murder. Jesus Christ was contented to ride on an Asse, the Apostles thought it no shame to goe barefoote: and we embrace gladlye, with reuerence their patience, humilitie, vertue, and mild manner in planting the Gospel. But you ride to preach on barbd horses, & put on the corselet not of faith, but of iron and steele, to set forward your strainge Religion. Al the world may see, that, as the maner and order of your procedinges is contrary to Christ, so all the stuffe ye vtter, is likewise contrary to his heauen-

heauenly Doctrine. what? Could ye
not ſuffer Martyrdome gladly for the
goſpel? No forſoth: ye choſe rather to ſlay
thē to be ſlaine, & no maruell. For ye loked for none other commoditie by your
Goſpel, but a loſeneſſe and liberty to liue
at your pleaſure. And therfore ſuch Goſpellers for ſuch a Goſpel were very loth
to leeſe their liues. The theefe wil neuer
gladly ſuffer deathe and ſpend his life in
defenſe of theft: for he purpoſeth to haue
none other frute and profite by theft, but
his ſweete life in this world maintained
at pleaſure. He that loſeth his life, ſayeth
Chriſt, preſerueth it into life euerlaſting:
but you were loth to loſe yours, for that
ye had no hope to haue any euerlaſting
life for it. Ye held it better to be Martyr-
makers, thē Martyrs: to do, then to ſuffer iniurie: Howbe it, to ſay the truthe,
ye ſuffred no iniury whē ye ſuffred death
for hereſy, for ye deſerued no leſſe. But,
when ye murdred other, ye did great iniury, whether they deſerued to die or no:
For that ye had no authoritye ſo to do.

Hold ſtil your hands a little while,
lay downe your Swordes and priuye
Dag=

Io. 12.

Daggers, let your fury coole, and harken to reason, and ye shall plainly perceiue, that there is great oddes betwene the order and due Ministration of Iustice, that the Emperoure and Christen Princes vsed to execute againste your wicked transgressions: and your impudent boldnesse, Traiterous Rebellion, and Bloudy Cruelty against Christendome. By the authority of God allmighty they beare the sword, and haue power to punishe the wicked: but, as for you, who made you, I pray you, rulers and Iudges in Israel? O vnhappy dayes, O wicked manners of our daies, maye we crye at this time with more iust occasion, then in his age Marcus Cicero did.

Rom. 13.

Bondslaues refuse to beare the yoke vnder their Maisters: Subiectes disdaine to obey the Commaundementes and Rule of their Magistrates, Theues would be Lordes and raigne ouer all. who be robbers, if you be Refourmers? Yea, who then shall be called Spoilers, Ennemies, Traitors, Tyrannes, and Cruell Bouchers, if you be Giltlesse and Innocentes?

To

To conclude in fewe wordes, what reaſonable cauſe doe ye alleage for your ſelues, why ye made warres ſo wicked and ſo abhominable, why ye prepared fire and ſagot to burne the whole world? was it becauſe ye were ſometimes burned for hereſie? Truly ye ſuffred not ſo muche nor ſo often as ye deſerued: but if perhaps, according to your deſertes, ye had gon oftner to the ſtake, yet ye ſhould haue ſuffred it patiently for the Goſpels ſake, if ye were Goſpellers (for ſo were the Apoſtles wont to do) at leaſt wiſe ye ſhoulde not haue reſiſted wyth force of armes, becauſe ye were ſubiectes, and were puniſhed by an order of law at the commaundement of the Magiſtrats and ſuperiour powers. Could not the freedome of your Goſpell floriſhe and purchaſe you the carnall freedome and looſe libertie of the fleſhe by no meanes without warre? In good ſoothe ye neded not to repine for lacke of libertie. For euery where ye were wont to ſet the vſuall and accuſtomed faſtes of þ Church at naught, and fill the Panche freely, to cary a ſiſter wife about with you, to toule Nunnes out

out of Cloysters, and with filthy and sacrilegious Lechery to abuse them: yea & most commonly every Apostate Monke had his Nunne at his taile. And so it agreed wel, if god wold haue had it so: for,

Holy Kate her holy mate,
And like his like must loue:
By holy trade, a broode is made,
To clime the Cloudes aboue.

It was the Frier Apostles pleasure, that his Lady Venus Court should be franke and free. If thy wife, saith he, wil not do it, let thy maide supply her place: the will of God commaundeth, and necessitie bindeth as wel to haue carnal copulation, and as to eat and drinke. Was it your drift to redresse the vitious liuing and loose maners of these daies? It had bene your part first to amend your owne selues, who were the worst in al y packe, and then hardely to lay to other mennes charge what ye could. Or was this your purpose to compell men to receiue your Gospell, and to poure it into their mouthes spite of their teethe? So did neuer Christ plant his Religion, but so Mahumet stablished his cursed sect. Ye labored

in

Sanctum sancta decet, his artibus i nr ad astra.

Lutheri Ep. ad Præpos. Luneburg.

in vaine, when ye trauailed to bring the world to your Religion by Uillany, railing and dubble Cannons , as eaſily as the Apoſtles did win men to the Goſpell of Chriſt, by their good liuing, preaching and miracles. How be it in dede, it was neither Religion, nor Goſpel, nor Gods quareil that ye ment to further: euen he him ſelf, who not for Gods ſake, but for malice againſt the Pope begã this whole Tragedy, is a currant-witneſſe in this poynt, and hath conſtantly ſo depoſed.

Was it to reſtore the Chriſten Faithe, (being as ye thoughte well nighe worne out) that ye made ſo great ſturre? Your labor was needleſſe: for the Churche of God, the Seat and ſure Piller of Truth, hath allwaies, without force and battail, moſt Reuerently and charely kepte the Faith that was from the beginning cõmitted to her Cuſtody. This Chriſt obtained of his Father: this ſhall the Heauenly Comforter the holye Ghoſte perfourm for euer. How thẽ good ſirs? was this wel done ſo to turmoile and toſſe the quiet ſtate and publike affaires of cõmon weales, to make a mixture and confuſion of whot and cold, high and low, to trou-

Luther began his goſpell for malice againſte the Pope, as he confeſſeth.
Ep. ad Argétin. impreſſ. Hagan. 1521.

1. Tim. 3.

Io. 17.
Io. 14.

ble and turne vp and downe all thinges
appertaining to God ♏ man, ſo lightly,
ſo raſhly, ſo wickedly without any iuſt
occaſion, without any ſufficient cauſe,
without any good reaſon?

Men that profeſſed Chriſtianity, haue
ſought cruelly and outragiouſly a longe
time againſt Chriſten men, haue ſought
their lines and goods, haue bereaued the
of houſe and home, of Church and Chappell: welthy and rich Cities are impone-
riſhed, ſacked ♏ ſpoiled, Church Veſtries
are voided, rifled ♏ robbed: And now if a
man call them to accomptes, ♏ aſke the
cauſe of al theſe their tragical ♏ cruel doings, he ſhal haue a ſhort anſwer to mum
budget, except they will peraduenture al-
lege this, ÿ the loſty Ambitiō, ÿ gredy Aua
rice, the deſperat boldnes of certen wicū
♏ loſe friers haue miniſtred iuſt occaſiō
of ſo horrible, wicked, ♏ hainous battel.

Now I come (moſt gentle Audiēce) to
ÿ ſecōd parte of this matter, to ÿ poynt
wherin I promiſed to make diſcourſe of
their cōſpiracies and treaſons: to the end
ye may plainly perceiue, ÿ our Aduerſaries were not only wout cauſe offded ♏
raſhli moued to bed their minds to fight,

2

but that also they toke weapon in hand, and bad battaile traiterously: and that as they attempted warre without iustice & right, so they proclaimed and pursued the same without Authoritye and Commission, to omit nothing that should help to fil vp the measure of their so great and execrable wickednesse.

3.

It is great pitye, in verye deede it is muche to be pitied, that Christen Princes doe make warre ofte against an other so often: yea and that, God wot, for light occasion, or wel nighe for none occasion at all. Desire of raigne and soueraigntie, a light displeasure taken vpon a word spoken, Glory, Hastinesse, Emulation of Rulers, haue bread vs many times long and cruell battaile, so that a man might wel now sing as the Poet Horace did.

Quicquid diliront Reges plectuntur Achiui.

When Kinges and Rulers kepe ill rule,
  The people paies for all:
Their ouersightes, the Commons sighes,
  And feeles their wanton fail.

The time shall come, Oh, I tremble when I speake it, the time shall come in deede, when it shall repent them to late, that by their lightnesse and raish panges,

fo much and fo manie mens blood hath
bene fhed . Yet to fay the truthe in fuche
warres, moft commonlie, the fouldiours
are excufed for that theyr part is rather
to obey, fulfil and accomplifhe their lawful Princes and Capitains commaundement, then deliberate, difpute and reafon
of the equitie of the caufe wherefore they
fight. But in this domefticall infurrecti-
on, in this moftruous Tumulte, and
Sedition, that hath bene fturred vp thefe
many yeres vnder pretenfe of refourmation in maters of Religion, wherein nor
Capitaine, nor Magiftrate , nor Prince,
nor Emperour biddeth any man ftrike:
where without anie Lieutenant general, knight Martial, or deputie Captaine
all the whole hofte is but an affemble of
priuate men , of common fouldiours , or
rather of rouers , cutthrotes and mofte
crnell murderers , who is voide of hainous offenfe? what one is free from ma-
licioufe treafon? who of all this companie is able to fay , that he is in his confcience giltleffe, innocent and vnfpotted?

Priuate men that had no Authoritie
at ail , bad battaill them felues of theyr

owne headdes, and ſtyckte not, without they? Kynge and Soueraigne his
commandement, to b?inge and receaue
into the Realme, fo?ayners, ſtraingers,
hy?ed ſouldioures and enemies.

I wyll aſke them nowe no mo?e,
what iuſte Quarell, what reaſonable
Cauſe they had, to muſter and to p?o-
clayme warre. Be it, that the Cauſe
was moſte iuſte and ſufficiente, becauſe
they? pleaſure was ſo: But this I aſke
them, what lawefull Power, what lawe,
what Statute, what Right, what Cuſtome o? common Example of Antiqui-
tie, what Autho?itie and Commiſſion
they had ſo to doe?

Whereas they are but mere P?iuate
men and Subiectes, called to no Office no? Autho?itie at all, no? placed in
anye roome o? Dignitie in the Common weale: yet they dare be ſo bolde,
as to Muſter, to Campe, to pytche a
Fylde, they take vppon them to my-
niſter Iuſtice, and right (right? Rather
may I cal it moſte vnmercifull w?onge)
they wyll needes be Rulers, yea and
rule al Rulers and the whole roſte them
                                            ſelues

selues alone.

If a man might be so bold as to aske you nowe , right Honorable Gospelinge Capytaines (as the Renoumed Prince and moste Reuerende Father my Lorde Cardinall of Lorraine a fewe yeres agoe asked the Ministers of that Deformed Churche in the Honorable Assemble at Poissie) wherehence came you? who sent you? By what Authoritie doe ye all these thinges? either ye shoulde be domme without any thing to saye (as they were then A longe whyle) Or lye impudentlye ; as your accustomed manner is : Or be driuen plainlye to confesse and graunte , that ye are but priuate Subiectes, of no Iurisdiction, of no Place or Degree, called to no Office or power to meddle with the Publyke Affaires of Christendome: Finally that (for all these your strainge, maruealouse, and monsterouse Mysteries which ye professe and practise moste impudently and desperately, takinge vppon you to redresse the state of all Christendome, and to Reforme matters of Religion) ye haue no Authoritye at all,

Who the after long deliberation answered, that his vocation was extraordinarie

D ij   neither

Neither ordinarie power in earth, nor extraordinarie Commiſſion from heauen. For ye ſhal neuer be able to proue either this by Miracles, or that by letters Patentes.

As for Martine Luther (or rather Luder, but that for ſhame he chaunged that filthie name of his) borne at Iſlibium in Saxonie, and begotten of a Sprite Incubus (as the common reporte goeth) who is your chiefe Apoſtell and Patriarche: we knowe him verie well, what he was, whence he came, and what authoritie he had. when he was a yonge man he ſtudied the ciuill law, and afterward when for his recreation he walked in the field nigh the Vniuerſitie of Erforde, he was ſtrykē down to ẏ grounde with a ſudden thunderclap and lighting, and his companion, that walked then with him, was with ẏ blow quite ſlaine before his face, whereat he was ſo aſtonied and put in ſuch feare, that he determined with him ſelf to forſake the world, to enter into Religion: & ſo out of hande made him ſelfe an Auguſtine Friere. At the laſte he was made Doctour in Diuinitie

Luder in the German tonge is as much to ſay as a ſlaue or a knaue. Vide Bú deriū in detect. Nugar. Luthe.

Fonta li. 1 Hiſtor. có. Sleid

nitie with shame inough: for he came to that degree with the money that was bequethed to an other man, whome, with the help of his Prior, he beguiled. what other estate or degree he had in the common weale, or Apostleship in the Church of God, beside this, we could neuer yet learne by any meanes. But in deede he braggeth verie often, that he is wel assured, that his doctrine and conclusions are from heauen, and that he was sent from heauen to the Germans to be their first Apostle that should preache them the Gospell: for before his dayes he sayed that they neuer had any true Religion or Christen doctrine. In few words he maketh more accompte of him selfe, then of S. Augustine and all other holie and auncient Fathers of Christes Churche.

This bragginge Thraso telleth manie strainge matters of him selfe more maruelouse then true. This is more like to be true as he reporteth of him selfe, that he had manie times familiar conference and talke with the Diuell. Yea and his Actes & doings during his raigne, written and faithfully regestred by Cocleus

D iij   and

Luther.
in ser de
destruct.
Hierus.
Luth. ad
ver falsò
nominat
stat. Eccl
& li côtr
Reg. An.

Luthli.:
de secul.
potest.

Luth. in
de Miss.
angu.

ᵱ other of his neighbours men of great learninge and credite, do most manifestly declare and proue, that from ᵹ diuel also his familiar frend & Prince of this world he receaued authoritie and commission to punish all good and honest men, and to gainesay and withstand the holy Masse.

Ihon Caluine borne at Nouiodunum in Picardie, a man banished frō his countreie for his wicked behauioure, and whiles he liued in his countreie, the veriest buthifte and naughtiest verlet of al his companions, first hydde him selfe at Basile, then beganne to shew his head at Straseburge and preache to the Renegates and Apostles there: At last came to Geneua, and put out the Deputie of the Citie, expelled the Bisshope and all the Cleargie that were honeste and Catholike, with all the vertuouse and substantiall Citysens, and so wanne Authoritie and beganne to raigne there like a Conquerer by the lawe of treason and force of armes.

What neede I here againe bring you in mind of that Epicure Beza the Burgonion, a Licentiate in law, who taketh

so much

Anton.
Democ.
de Missæ
sa. c.2.
Ioā. Va-
querius
lib de
Tentat.

Vide
Lindani
Dialogū
inscript.
Dubitat.
Fol 139.

so muche Poeticall licence, that in his bawdie and sylthie Epigrammes he passeth farre the wanton Pagan Poetes Martiall, and Tibullus? what shall I speake of Bernardinus Ochinus ý Italiane, who laboreth to plante the beastly Doctrine of Polygamie, that is, that more then one wife at once may ioyne to a man in ý state of lawful matrimony, willing therefore and perswadinge men to be Manywiuers, as the Turkes are.

what shall I tell you of Peter Martyr the Renegate Moncke, or of Bernarde Rotman an vnlearned Asse that beganne to professe learninge, and by color of only Scripture, whiche he vnderstode not, expelled the Catholikes out of the Citie of Munster? Or of Ihon of Leid ý tailor, ý furiouse captaine of the mad Anabaptistes, who, within a yeare after, got ý vpper hand of Rotman, draue out ý Lutherans, brought in ý Anabaptistes bega to raigne in ý very same Cit, hauing won & conquered ý field by ý same crafte & pretese of scripture only, as Rotmã did before, & so gaue him a fall in his own turn & serued him to his own sauce?

D iiij or

or of Oſiander that Holie Man commonlye called the ſeconde Enoch, a Goddes name, or of Caroloſtadius that rude maried Archedeacon of wittemberge, who became afterwarde for mere ſoly a mad and vnſkilful plowghman, to the wonder and laughinge game of all that coūtry. Or of Illyricus, Muſculus, Farellus, Virettus? Or of Bucer, Morot and Malot, the ringleaders and teachers of all miſchefe? good God, what a table haue we here, what a noble ranks of vertuous, graue & renoumed Fathers is here? ſuch as I aſſure you, no honeſt and diſcreete houſeholder woulde euer ſuffer by his good will to tarie within his doores.

Such Champions are they that profeſſe them ſelues to be the Aduerſaries and enemies of the Catholike Churche? theſe be ẙ captains that ſtand againſt the Biſſhopes of Chriſtes Church, ẙ kinges of Chriſtendome and Rulers of cōmon weal es. Such are the Oratoures and Preachers that vſe to declaime, to raile, to thunder againſte the blood & Shrines of Martyres, againſt the Catholyke and
vniuer-

vniuersal Religion of the Christians, a=
gainst the mystical and holy Sacramen=
tes of the Churche: Yea and sticke not,
like madde dogges, to barcke and baye
against ᵽ very blessed and pretiouse body
of our Lord Iesus Christ. These, yea such
fellowes as these be, are they who nowe
these manie yeres, vsurpe a Lordly au=
thoritie ouer vs, whome we are compel=
led to take for our masters, who take vp=
pon them to controlle the doinges and
maners of all the whole world: And yet
can we learn by no meanes wherehence
came this so Imperiall a soueraigntie,
or who gaue them so greate and princely
Authoritie: except we say they had it of
Satan, and ᵽ they be the very vndouted
prophets and Forerunners of Antichrist.

The Bysshoppes and Prelates of
Christes Church doe excommunicate the
put their flocke, and seperate them from
the mystical Society, felloship and Com=
munion of all Christian men. The Chri=
sten Princes and Rulers of the worlde
do bannissh them, do take them for out=
lawes, and both by proclamations and
force of armes trauaile with much care
and

and diligence, to defende and ſaue them ſelues and theyr louing Subiectes from them: God allmightie the Omnipotent Lord and Ruler of heauen and earth neuer ſignifyed to the worlde by any miracle, Signe, or ſeely token, that we ſhoulde take ſuche as theſe are for hys Commiſſioners or Deputies: excepte a man will ſaye, that this is a Miracle, y theſe fellowes oftentymes (whyles in the preſence of the People, they fains that they are able, in the Uertue of the Goſpel they preache, to reſtore the dead to lyfe) dor make the liue ſtark dead, as a certaine Preacher did, one Mathias in Polonia, and the like is crediblie reported of Ihon Caluine at Geneua.

Howe then? what ſhal we take them to be? In fewe wordes, they are theeues that come in by the windowe, they are Murderers, Traytours, Heretykes, Satans Miniſters. For why, theyr doeinges declare no leſſe. They doe the Commons wronge, they conſpire againſte Princes, they diuide the Churche with Sectes, they prouoke God hym ſelfe with horrible Blaſphemie. By flacterie,

terie, and bearinge themselues a lofte like graue bearded goates they currie fauor with the fimple people, and studie to be in credit with ý Cōmons & baseſt ſort, by clawing them where they itche, and telling thē faire tales of liberty, loosenes and light burdens, such as they know the people are glad to heare. Otherwise in verie dede they haue nothing to do with such affaires as they meddle wal. They can neuer beare out themselues by any law of God or man, for takinge vpon thē the office and profeſſion of Refourminge Religion, nor excuse them selues by any meanes frō hauing don to much amiſſe, and moſt greuouſe wrong, in that they toke weapon in hand and made war.

For they, being but priuate mē, yea & ý ý moſt vile, base, & worſte of al men, in raʒing choler & furiouſe madnes, did ſtād vp, gainsay and reſiſte the lawes and magiſtrats, did ſturre thē ſelues & others againſt theyr Chriſtiā Emperors, kings, & rulers, did ſeperat thēſelues from the compani of al honeſt & faithful ſubiectes, did bid battail to their owne natiue coūtry, did reioyce & triumph in their wicked and rauing theeuerie.

O God immortall, howe many, howe greate and hainouſe treſpaces are here couched together in this one wicked and curſed attempt? The natiue borne ſigheth againſt his owne countreie, one fellow ſtriketh at an other, the ſonne ſmiteth his Father, the ſubiecte aſſaulteth his Gouernour, the Souldiour turneth the edge of his ſworde againſt his owne Captain, one Chriſtiã purſueth an other Chriſtian with deadlie blowes, with gunnepouder and fire: finallye mortall man prouoketh euerliuinge God with miſchiſe, wickednes and blaſphemies.

O moſte mercifull and higheſt Lorde God of heauen, to what vnhappie dayes haſt thou brought and reſerued vs, that we ſhould liue & ſee this miſerable tyme and lamentable age? what caſe, what order, what ſtate, what face of a Chriſtian common weale is this? Lawes, Magiſtrates, right cã bear the ſway no where, y Royall Scepter & Mace of the Empire lieth donne on the grounde, the ſacred crownes of Chriſten kinges are trodden vnder traitors feete: It is lawfull and right for euery deſperate ſhakebuckler to

doe

đor what he liſte, and his liſte is to doe, that his bealy biddes him, that pryde pricks him, that madnes cōmandes him.

De is takē to be the iolieſt fellow and to haue beſt profited in the libertie of the Goſpell, who feareth nothing, who ſetteth by no man, who thinketh him ſelſe bounde to obey no law at all. what can be more tediouſe and troblouſe, more vnrulie and outragiouſe, more horrible, execrable, terrible, in that Jnfernal depe Pyt of Satan, amonge the vgly diuelles of hell themſelues then this, that euery bodie coueteth rule & to be maſter ouer other, and none can abyde obedience, and to be a quiet ſubiect? That al things are done in a confuſe tumulte, nothinge aduiſedly and in order ? That the higheſt and loweſt without diſtinction are mingled and ruffled together? that colde and heate, drowthe and moiſture ſtriue and contend with continual diſcord, and contrarietie one with an other?

Pardon me, I beſeche you (moſt gentel Audience) pardon me, if perhappes this quicke and egree talke ſeeme in your learned eares ouer bitter and loth-
ſome

ſome. If I ſpeake home & moꝛe freely, thē
ran well agree with your milde and gentle natures, it may pleaſe your goodneſſe
to haue me excuſed, and lay the blame, as
reaſon is, on them whoſe wicked demea-
nure compelled me thus to ſpeake: whoſe
deepe and feſtered woundes can not be
healed with lenitiues and temperate me-
dicines: whoſe greuous ſoꝛes and abhominations cã not be declared with milde
and gentle language.

For what can be oꝛ ſpoken to bitterly,
oꝛ don to ſeuerely againſt thē, who with
theyꝛ wicked and curſed mouths do raſſe
rage, and cal the moſt renoumed & noble
Chꝛiſtian Kinges and Pꝛinces, ſlaues,
bouchers, knaues, and the Reuerende
Biſhopes (Chꝛiſtes moſt holy Uicars)
Antichꝛiſts, bawdes, Iſldeꝛ who ſtick
not to publiſhe in theyꝛ wꝛitinges, that
the great Turk is ten times beter, wiſer,
& honeſter mã, thē our Chꝛiſtian Rulers
& Pꝛinces? who beare men earneſtly in
hãd, ꝑ no mã, except he wil be Satãs own
childe, ought to obey ꝑ woꝛthy & ꝛe itcꝰ
decree of ꝑ moſt noble Empeꝛoꝛ Charles
the fiſte ꝑ he pꝛoclaimed at Woꝛmes by ꝑ
                                    while

Margin notes:

La. gloſ.
ad Edic.
Imperi.
& in ad-
moni. ad
Germ.
ſuos teu
tonicè
ſcript.

Luth. ad
uerſ. exe
crab. An
tichriſti
Bullam.
Lib. cõt.
prætenſ.
ſtat. Ecc.

Lu. cont.
duo mã-
dat. Cæſ.

Lu. gloſ.
ad Edic.
Imper.

aduise & consent of ye Princes & estates of Germanie for ye appeasing of seditio, & ye quenching of dangerouse contention in maters of Religion.

These be but trifles & light maters in coparison of ye rest of this theyr wicked & traiterouse cospiracie. In the very honorable presēce & hearing of our Late soueraigne Charles ye fifte, & ye estates of the Empire at wormes, the worthie third Elias, out of those words of our Sauiour Christ in the Gospel (I came not to send peace, but the sword) concluded, that it ought to be a thinge to be wished for as moste acceptable to Christen men, and speciallie to him, that strife and contētion should rise and growe aboute the word of God. Yea, not longe after, he dydse set out to the sight and vew of the whole world seditious and Heretical Bookes, wherein he did the best he coulde to abolishe all due obedience, to abrogate all Policie and Ciuile gouernment, to perswade the People to rebel and forsake theyr Spirituall and Temporall Rulers and Masters, to prouoke them to steelinge & robbinge, to bludshed and

murder

Vide dia.
secun.
Dubita
iij. p. 278

Refert
Geor.
Wiceli-
us in ret.
Luthe-
ranifmi.

murder, to facking and burning of hou-
fes, of Cities, of Churches.

He faied, that men fhould waifhe their
handes in ỹ bloud of ỹ Romifh Clergie.
He affirmed in his writinges, that it was
ỹ very true nature & cõplexiõ of ỹ gofpel

Epift. ad
Frat. inf.
Gier.

to moue and fturre vp war and fediti-
on: That there ought to be no Magiftrate, no fuperiour at all amonge Chrifte
men: That men ought to pray God ear-

li. de pot
feculari.

neftlie, that it would pleafe him to put in
the headdes of the vplandifh men of Germanie, not to obeie theyr Princes, nother

lib. cont.
duo edi.
Cæfaris.

to goe to warre with them againfte the
Turke: That men fhould contribute nothing towardes the charges of the warre
againft the Turk: That it was not law-

li. de bel
lo cont.
Turcam.

full for Chriften men to warre againfte
the Turke, but that they fhould fuffer
and beare patiently and with a good wil
all violence, wronge, and iniury that
were done to them. Yea that it was fo
farre againft the lawe of God to fight a-

Luth. af-
fert. ar-
ticul. 24.

gainft the Turke, that if anie man fhould
be fo hardie as to doe it, it might be well
fayed, that he fought againfte God him
felfe, and feemed to repine and refifte
againfte

againste his heauie hand and iuste punishement: That neither man nor Angel of heauen had anie Authoritie at all to make anie law or one syllable, whereto Christen men should be bound to obey, more or longer then it pleased them. For we are, saied he, franck and free from all things. And in case anie thing were decreed and laied on the neck of a Christen man, wherto he should be of necessitie constrained to obey againste his will and consent, that that proceded of tyrannie, & should be taken for violéce and crueltie: finally that there was no hope of redresse and reformation, except the lawes and decrees of all men were vtterlie abolished, and the free Gospell of libertie called home again, according to the whiche all things should be iudged, ruled and gouerned.

With these strainge opinions and singular Paradoxes the fundation of the fift Gospell was laied, and hence consequentlie the springes and grasses of this wicked conspiracie and treason, we talke of, began to budde.

When Thomas Muntzer, this Euan-

Lib. de capt. Babil.

Thou Luther being the if preacher of that Gospell wold haue been king alone hus self.

E   gea

Touching thisinsurrection of Muntzer reade Cocleus de act. Luth. Anno. 1525.

gelistes scholer, had learned thies highe Mysteries of his master, he began to preache apace, he made manie seditiouse sermons to the people, exhorted them to diuide them selues from ẙ Catholike Churche, to forsake their Magistrates & Rulers, & to shrinke away from them, sent his letters about the countreie, gathered a great hoste of vplandysh Paisantes, of most wicked persones, of desperate slaues, & out of hand biddeth battaille. who biddeth it? (good God) and againste whome? will ye see who it is? forsooth it is Thomas Muntzer the Apostle of Saxonies scholer, a man that should haue bene bound in chaines, according to ẙ counsel of the learned physition Hyppocrates, for his madnes, a monstruouse, contagiouse and pestilent beaste, framed and made of all maner of stinkinge vices and sylthie ordure, that biddeth warre againste his owne countreie Germanie (a noble Countrie sometime & most florisshing) againste Princes & Rulers, againste ẙ verie Churche of God himself.

Oh wicked villaine, oh pestilent monster

ter, oh curſed Rakehell. Yea and the impudent Captif was not aſhamed to call it alſo, the battaille of the lord. For ſo he tried to his ſouldiours: fight good brethern, fight manfullie the lords battaille, ſigt Gods field. For he ſaied, he had commiſſion by Gods own mouth, to bid battaille againſt all Princes & Kinges. The verie ſame ſaied Luther alſo, affirming ꝑ God him ſelf did riſe & ſtand againſte the eſtates of Germanie & theyr tyrannie: That it was the lyuing God of heauen his own proper battaille, and not the poore Paiſantes of ꝑ countreie: and withall the lieng Prophete aſſured moſt conſtantly before hand by his falſe ſprite of Prophecie, that the Rebelles of the countreie ſhould ſuerlie haue the vpper hand, and that the Princes and Nobles ſhould be vndone, haue ꝑ ouerthrow and vtter deſtruction.

Well nowe, Muntzer then goeth forwarde verie luſtilie and deſperatelie with his Vplandyſhe Souldioures, of whome he had a meruelouſe greate number aſſembled about him, and laboreth tothe and naile what he could, to

Melanc.
commēt.
ad Col.

wring the ſword out of the magiſtrates handes, to depriue them of al authoritie, power and rule, to degrade and depoſe them from all honor, dignitie and Princelie eſtate.

Manie a notable Caſtle and Palais, manie a goodlie Abbey and Churche was quite raſed and ouerthrowen by his wicked meanes and doinge: yea in onlie Franconia, as ſomme men write, no leſſe then three hundred.

Eraſ. Alberus & Conrad. Wimp. lib. contra Suinglium.

Upon this at Franckford two noble Captaines, a tailor and a ſhomaker, beganne to ſtrike vp alarme to a freſhe rebellion, to blow the trompet, to call their ſouldiours to the field. They ſhutte the toune gates, appointed new companies and Aldermen of the wardes, made election of new Senators and counſellers, ſomoned a parlemēt, and ordained new lawes, expelled thofficers & magiſtrats out of the toune, ſome they butcherlie murdred, ſent their ſtatute bookes to other Cities, to ſtirre vp other to ſedition, & to take weapon by theyr example.

Herevpon at Mogunce, at Kincauia, at Colen: Herevppon in all quarters of Germanie

Germanie suche a tumult, suche an insurrection, suche an vproze is sturred vp, suche a terrible and traiterouse rebellion is by and by risen, as neuer the traitor Catiline attempted the like in Rome. The whole world is sett a fire with the heate of this Gospel. manie puissant, renowned and notable personnes of the nobilitie are cruellie murdred, emong whome the honorable Earle of Helsensteine was one. who, as it is reported, was forced to runne vpon their pikes. All things, high and low, are turned vpsidedown, deadlie warre rageth on euerie side, horrible feare raigneth euerie where. For whie? the lordes and Rulers were now more afraied of their own subiectes & seruantes, then of their soraine enemies and strangers. But yet at laste by th'ayed mercy and benefite of God almightie, the victorie stode on the Nobles side: who ouercame the Paisantes, toke Muntzer (who repented greuouslie his wicked & traiteronse doings and at laste loste his head) and slew in y space of thzee monethes a hundzed and thyztie thousand of the Rebelles.

Erasmus Alber: reported it.

E iij   what

what did our woꝛthie Col Pꝛophet
then, who befoꝛe by his falſe Pꝛophecie
gaue ẏ ouerthꝛow and vtter deſtruccion
to the Nobles,and gaue the conqueſte
and victoꝛie to his ſouldiours of the
countree? It is likelie, that here the ſecond Ieremié, (foꝛ he can quicklie beare
the perſone of whiche Pꝛophete he liſte)
ſate ſolitarie,weeping and lamenting
the calamitie and miſerable caſe of his
countreie. Verilie and ſo he did. Foꝛ
then he caſte awaye foꝛ verie anguyſhe
of mynd his friers cote, and betakes
himſelf to his nunne Katherine Booꝛe,
one of thoſe it. whiche his bawd Leo-
nard Knoppen ſtale out of ẏ Nunnerie
of Nimyke on good friday,when Chꝛiſten men vſe to celebꝛate the memoꝛie of
Chꝛiſtes bleſſed and bitter paſſion.

 This woman,after ſhe had ben well
bꝛoken ⁊ framed two yeres with wanton toyes and lecherouſe recreations
among the ſcholers of wittenberge ,the
pooꝛe ſeelie ſoꝛie man taketh in his armes , ⁊ foꝛ verie heauineſſe ⁊ griefe em-
bꝛaceth her patiétlie,⁊ kiſſeth her denoue
ly ⁊ ful oſten w̃ al his hart. Yea he toke
        it

Luthers
mariage,
Anno.
1525.

it no scorne to daunce and drink Carous and refuse not, though he was a Frier to marie a Nunne, which was a strainge matter and neuer hard of before, and all for verie penance & sorow to see so great murder and so muche bloudshed: whereof himself was the only cause & Author.

It is without fayle a meritoryouse deed, as the Cannons saye, to take a whoore out of the stewes and marie her to make her an honest woman : and he toke an honest woman out of a Nunrie to marie her & make her a whoore. So in doing his penance he missed but a litle, being ouerseen in taking quid p quo one thing for an other. And withall, this Apostolick point was to be noted in this Holie Prophete, that out of hand, as the wind and flattering blast of fortune turned, so he turned his saile, chainged his style, sung an other song, and wrote bitterlie againste the poore vplandish men when he saw them ouercomme, yealded them to Satan, and committed them as gyltie and worthie to die to the edges of the Magistrates swordes. Yea he reuiled them & railed at them, ca'ling them di=

Luth.
contra
cohort.
Rustic.

E iij   nelles

nelles of hell, and ſaied that out of dout
the Nobles might eaſelie winne heauen
by ſhedding the bloud of ſuch traiterous
rebelles.

See, I pray you, the Euangelical
ſprite of this Apoſtle, how dubble it is,
how experte and readie in falſe fayning
and diſſimulation. All this he wrote to
make the world beleue, that he was
none of that pack and wicket conſpiracie of rebelles: wheras in deed he was ye
Author and Grandcaptaine that did ſet
them on, and clapte his handes and eg-
ged them forward, as long as they had
anie hope to haue the vpper hand.

Teſte
Stolſio
i ſom-
nio
Luth. &
in defen-
ſione.

We maye thank this traiteronſe Catiline of our time, for all theſe blouddie
tragedies. By ſuche practizes he came in
fauor with Solimam the great Turke,
in whoſe Bokes he was highelie esteemed: & wel worthie ſo to be. For by occaſion of debate about ye Lutheran Goſpell, and ſo through Luthers meanes, he
conceaued Good hope to ouerrunne and
conquer all Germanie, when he came to
that Keye of Chriſtendome ye noble Citie Vienna Auſtriæ, with ſuche a huge
great

The
Turkes
brag that
two hun-

great hoſt, ý he made all Europe quake.
Yea Soliman wrote in plaine wordes
that he wiſhed Luther long life, that
he hoped the daie ſhould come, that Lu=
ther ſhould find him his good maſter.
And in verie deed at that time the terrible and mortall enemie of Chriſtendome
gaue a great puyſhe, & miſſed but a litle
to ſubdue al Germanie, whiles Chriſten
men, being at debate betwen them ſelues about the Goſpell, drew curtiſie verie vncourteouſlie, and were in doubt
whether they ſhould go with the Emperour & fight againſte him or no, had not
God of his infinite mercie then eſpeciallie holpen his afflicted flocke and ſpared
his people.

   I can not woout great greif of harte
remember, ý by the wicked meanes and
procurement of this Goſpeller, one of ý
beſte Chriſten Emperours ý euer ruled
Chriſtendome, was brought in trouble
and great danger among his own ſubiectes. As there anie man aline, ý euer
ſaw, or can anie of vs all call to remembrance, ý we euer hard or read of ſuch a
Noble & worthy Prince for wit, vertue,

F b   mon=

died and
fortie
thouſand
as it is re
ported by
Gaſpar
Hedio
Hiſt.
Synop.
ad Sa-
bell.

Teſto
Ioanne
Manlio
in loc.
comun.
to.j. Fc.
195.

prowesse, experience, courage, and for al
other Princely graces, honorable giftes,
and renoumed actes, as was our late
puissante & mightie Emperoure Charles the fifte? Yea this Princelie man, this
Lieutenant general, Patrone, and De-
fendor of all Christendome, this moste
renoumed Emperour was assaulted and
entrapped by this pestilent treason and
Gospelissh conspiracie. And whereas it
should haue become Germanie espe-
ciallie to obey him at a beck : certaine
Germans mustered, made a great hoste
& all the power they could againste him,
and pursued him in open warre (whiche
they call Smalcald Fielde) thoughe,
(thankes be to God) they loste the field
and preuailed not.

Smal-
cald field.

I could here tell you of the greate
Sedition and insurrection in Zuitzerlād
whiche was sturred vp by Zuinglius,
the raging flame whereof was so fearce
and great, that the blond of manie thousand men was scarse able to quenche it.

The in-
surrection
of the Hel
uetians
sturred vp
by Zuin-
glius, An-
no. 1 5 3 1.
Cronic
Germa.

I could declare vnto you, how the
traiterouse Gospellers of England gathered a maine hoste againste their moste
ver=

vertuouse ladie Queene Marie the rare treasure, ỹ peerlesse Iewell ỹ moste perfecte Paterne & Example of our daies. How they shotte arrowes and Dartes againste her Courte gates, conspired her death, deuised to poison her, to kil her with a dagge at one time, w a priuie dagger at an other time, reuiled her, called her bastard, boutcher, printed seditiouse bokes againste her, wherein they railed at her like Hellhoundes, and named her traiterouse Marie, mischeuouse Marie.

wiates
Rebellion

knokes
bokc.

It were to long to rehearse, how the noble Queene of Scotland that now raigneth, was driuen a great while to liue like a poore priuat woman in her own realme, to obey her own subiectes, & to doe no more then they gaue her leaue: yea, and in the meane tyme was euerie daye and euery houre in greate peril & danger of her life among them.

I need not tell, that euery man knoweth, how the Gentell men that were seduced by thies new preachers rebelled againste their Prince in Suecia: no, how ỹ Comōs made an vproze againste their king in Denmarck.

But

But I can not omit, to ſpeake of that late treaſon and cruell conſpiracie of the Hugonoes in Fráce, who could withoute weeping teares abyde to tell, how thoſe naughtie, falſe & wicked ſubiectes were not aſhamed, to ſtand in open field againſte their own natural Soueraigne in his own realme? To bid war and fight againſte theyr lawfull King, during his Nonage, to make a leagne and confederacie wᵗʰ y̓ enemies of his croune, to ſell his Cities and townes to forayners & ſtraingers for mony? This holie bataille (for the Goſpell & Gods name) was fought againſte France by Frenchemen themſelues: that is, firſt by Caluin the Dictator and General of the field, then by Beza the Lieutenant, and Othomannus and Spiſamius the petie Captaines. Theſe were the cheiſe doers in deed, though as they toke the coloure of Religion & pretenſe of reſourmatiou for cloke of their treaſon, ſo they vſed the names & ſeruice of certaine of y̓ nobilitie of France whome they had ſeduced to beare out the brunte of the Battaille, the ſmarte of the ſtrokes, the enuie, the
infamie

infamie, & all the outward face and porte
of that busy mater. These were the
Knaues that lay in ý stocke: as for other,
they were but theyr trumping Cardes.

The preface of their tragedie was verie calme and peaceable. They would
seeme to go verie orderlie to work. They
got an edict to be made forsooth for the
furtherance of theyr Gospell, they got a
law by force and extorsion against ý king
and Magistrats wil and pleasure. The Clau̅d.
highe Court of Parlement of Paris made D.Sain&
answer at the firste, We can not, we wil du Sac-
not, we ought not. But afterward they cag.Fo
were compelled to let the bill passe, & the 58.
Edicte of Januarie to be made, ý these
rakehels might preach without ý walles
by permission, and as it were by vertue
of a law : which: law to all honest good
men neuer seemed worthie to haue the
name of a law, as the whiche was obtained by force, was laied vppon mens
neckes by the might and violence of
theeues and traitours that had taken &
bound ý Common weale hand & foote,
was written and penned against all
reason and equitie. But yet a law they
would

would needes haue , were it neuer so
vnlawfull , to be a cloke to couer theyr
outragiouse sedition.

And in deed at the firste they made
them selues verie humble and meeke,
when the King and the Honorables of
Fraunce were assembled about weightie
& greate affaires of ye Realme at Poissie,
thither came the twelue Apostles of that
deformed Churche , of whiche number
eight or nyne were Apostates, Munkes,
and friers that had caste of their habites,
broken their vowes , and forsaken theyr
profession: suche smothe marchantes, ye in
outward talke and worde, in the presence of that honorable Audience , would
speake of nothing, but of peace and concord , of good faith and simple dealing:
whereas in deed they meante , they minded, they wrought nothing els, but wicked conspiracie and treason, but sacking
of churches, burning of cities, murdring
of Citisens , and the vtter ruine and de-
struction of that Realme. Yet that they
were so earnest to haue a law for theyr
syde, and by publike authoritie to be suffred to preache after their cursed fashion,
their

their intent and purpoſe therein was this : that vnder pretenſe of a law they might vndoe the realme, and turne the King out of his kingdom , as they did before vnder colour of the word of God, expell the Biſſhops wellnighe out of the Churche.

wold you haue a law , that refuſe to liue vnder a law ? who is ſo blind ẙ can not plainlie ſee , that your craſte & practiſe is, to driue out (as it were) one naile with an other: whiles vnder the ſhadow of Religion and law , ye labor what ye can, to banniſhe all law & Religion out of the world, to ouerthrow the Churche, to roote all ciuill order and policie of tēporall affaires out of all Chriſten Realmes, countreis and Cities ?

But I pray you , by what law made you that wicked conſpiracie, when ye agreed together to robbe & ſpoile in one night all ẙ Churches in France at ones, if all things had framed & fallen out according to your phanſies & purpoſe euerie where , as they did in Gaſcoine & diuers other places of France , where according to the appointement the matter was

Claud. D. Sainctes du ſaccag. Fo. 55.

was put in practice in deed with moſt
deſperate boldnes, and wicked Sacrilege? By what Religion or law did a
great companie of you flock together at
Challon in Burgundie, & there in your
Conuocation houſe made a Synodalle
decree, that euerie man ſhould endeuor
to his power to driue three Vermines
out of Chriſtendome, the Churche of
Rome, the Nobilitie, the publike order
of iuſtice? If ye denie it, your names are
to be ſeen yet in the Recordes of the
highe Court of Parlement at Paris,
where manie of you were accuſed for it
by the Rulers and eſtates of Burgundie.

The
three
eſtats of
Burgun-
die do re-
porte this
in the ſe-
cond part
of theyr
Diſcours
vpon the
Frenche
Kings
Edict.

when ye trauayled vnder a pretenſed
ſhew of Gods worde to diſſanull and
aboliſhe the Supremacie of the chiefe
Biſſhop of the Chriſtiãs, who according
to the commiſſion and charge geuen vnto
him by Chriſtes owne mouth, vſed euer
to feed & rule bothe the ſheep and lambes
of Gods flocke: then were theſe wordes
euer in your monthes, Honour the king,
1.Pet 3.
Tit.3.
obey the king as the higheſt: warne them
to hearken and obey Princes and Rulers.
But when ye conſpired and agreed together

gether at Geneua like villaines & traitours, to find priuie meanes, when time,
place, and occasiō might serue you, to rid
out of the waie and murder the late vertuouse and good king of France Fraun-
cis the second, the Queene his wife (who
now, God be thanked, hath gotten the
vpper hand ouer the rebelles and raigneth in Scotland) the Queue Mother,
her children, all the nobles, and all the
Catholike and good Officers of Fraunce:
where was then your scripture and that
accustomed sentence of yours, Honoure
the Kinge?

Out of all doubt you meane nothinge
els by these wordes, but to thruste your
sword through the Bisshoppes body in
to the Kinges harte. It was your Po-
lycie first to vanquish the Bishop by the
worde, that ye might the more easely afterward kill the King with the sword.

But here perhappes some one will
aske, howe I knowe all this? To him I
make this answer, that this is set out in Defens.
printe in Fraunce vnder the Kings pu- Reg. &
nilege: and therefore seing it is cōmon Relig.
in euerie mans hand, knowen to al men Fol. 16.

and ſet out to the ſight of the worlde in
defenſe of the moſte Chriſtian King and
of the Catholike Religion, it can not be
vnknowẽ, alſo to me. Yea & may it pleaſe
him to vnderſtãd, that I know this alſo
that I read and ſaw with my owne eyes
ý laſte yeare at Orleans, I meane a libel
printed in ý name of all ý Hugonots of
Fraunce to theyr Soueraigne Lorde
and King, wherein was nothinge ells
from the beginning to the ending, but
impudent boldnes, deſperate threatnin=
ges, and ſhameful treaſon.

The ſubiettes were not afrayed to
write to theyr King, ý he could not raign
ouer thẽ, that they would ſuffer his yoke
and obey his commaundement no lon=
ger, excepte he would be contented to
rule his realme in ſuch ſort, and by ſuch
lawes and ordinances, as they ſhould
appointe him. That they plaied the
very fooles, when by his commaunde=
mente they layed doune theyr weapons:
that they woulde ſurely take them in
hand againe, excepte he woulde looke
well to hymſelfe, and putte out of the
Councell of Paris certaine noble and
Hono=

Honorable men, who as they ſayed, were theeues Rouers, Butchers: and place in theyr romes certains of theyr brethren in Chriſte.

what coulde be ſpoken or inuented more Proudelye, more Impudently, more ſeditiouſlie, and malitiouſly, then that they vttered in this malaperte, ſtubborne, and traiterouſe Libell? The Printer of Orleans was kepte and feaſted a fewe dayes with the Officers of that Toune in theyr houſes, in ſtede of a Priſon, for printinge this Oration: and y̆ was al that was done to him then for it.

with the lyke Spirite one Goodman an Engliſſhe man, an earneſte and hotte Preacher of this Goſpell, for a grudge and malice he bore againſte his Soueraigne Ladie and Myſtreſſe Marye the moſte hyghe and Honorable Queene of Englande, dydde ſette out a monſtruouſe Booke in deede a fewe yeares agoe againſte the monſtruouſe Raygne of women, as he ſayed: yea, the impudente, vile, and ſhameleſſe villaine

Goodmás boke againſte y̆ monſtruousraigne of womē.

F ij   Trai

Traitor called that moſte noble and vertuouſe woman Proſerpine (whome the Poetes faine to be Queue of hel) and for her ſake gathering choler and ſtomake againſt all women, he railed at them all, and reuiled them, & like a common ſcolde would by his wil ſet on a cookinge ſtole, all the whole flocke and generation of woman kinde.

He ſaied it was neither law, nor right, nor reaſon, that any woman ſhould be a Ruler and ſyt in the Princelie Seate of any Common weale: that it might well ſeeme a monſtruouſe rule, and contrarye to nature, if men were compelled to obey a woman: if wome were ſuffred to beare the ſway and gouerne the publike eſtate of any kingdome.

If he wrote thus eſpecially for hatred and malice he bare againſte women, he ſwarued much from the common and accuſtomed manner and faſſhion of his fellowes, who doe atribute ſo much to women, and are of ſuche a fonde and filthie opinion, that they thinke it impoſſible for a man to liue one daye without the companie of a woman, Howbeit in deed they
be

be naughtie and lewde women, fit and ready to the game only, that these fellowes loue so much: but as for good women (among whome this vertuouse Queene might be wel Quene & Princesse in dede) they can not abide, but doe vtterly detest them, and hate them as muche as they hate all good men.

Out of doubt in one thing this Gospeller obserued iumpe y wonted practise and beate path of his companions: that vnder pretense of speaking againste women he endeuored to sturre the people to rebellion, and the subiectes to shrinke away and forsake theyr liege and lawful Soueraigne. And thys is euen the very daily and common custome of all the packe of such new Gospellers & Reformers, who caste theyr platte and are fully set, be it right or wrong, by foraine battayle abrode, or by rebellion at home, to trouble and disquiete the peaceable state & good order of al common weales, when it seemeth their turne they are so skilful, y they can put in vre both these mysteries of their Gospell at ones.

when the Emperour of worthie me-

F iij morie

morie Charles the fifte was entangled and troubled at Oeniponte with theyr tumulte and rebellinge, Soliman the Greate Turke was in the meane tyme requested in theyr behalfe to make war,

Defenf. Staphil. contr. Il. Et Sleid. notat.

for the furtherance and Defense of theyr fifte Gospell. The greate Turke, I saye (Oh horrible & most impious acte) was sent for, that whyles they assaulted the Emperour and kepte hym at a bay in Germanie, Budensis Bassa the Turkes Deputie should sette vppon his brother Ferdinande in Hungarie. The letters of that Conspiracie were taken: so that theyr crafte herein is open, theyr falshode can not be denied, theyr wickednes and treason can by no coloure be couered or cloked.

It were an infinite matter (gentell Audience) that might be here alleged, if I would reckon vp all these Gospellers traiterouse enterpriſes, and make full diſcours of euery particular parte of theſe haynouſe Conſpiracies. For in deede they haue lefte nothinge vndone that anie cruell Robbers, falſe Traitours, or wicked Heretikes, could euer com-

committe, attempte or deuise againste all good men, against Princes, against God allmightie himselfe. They haue iniured and traiterously offended the Royall maiestie of all the Kings and Princes of Christendome, they haue disturbed, impaired, and broken all politike order and rule of all Common weales. They haue disquieted, vexed and disordered the high Courte of the Imperiall Chamber, they haue abolished ye auncient lawes and customes of the Emperours Supreme Consistorye, and haue appointed newe of theyr owne makinge, so that Iustice and Ryghte is bannisshed from thence: in suche sorte that there remayneth scarse anye Signe or token of Lawe and Equytie in that renoumed place, and Imperall benche. for it ys theyr pleasure that all thinges be tried & decided by fyere and and sworde. Yea and what say ye by this, that many bookes and Lybells of theyrs haue bene commonly found and seen abroade, wherein they vttered theyr studie & declared theyr attempt & trauaile to alter and chainge al ye order of iustice & iudgementes of the

This writteth Brunus de Hæro. lib. 2.

F iiij   Em-

Empire, to take awaye and abrogate all the Ciuill Lawes, and to make a new Policie and Order of gouernement of theyr owne phantaſticall deuiſe.

And it was not inough in theyr opiniõ, nor ſufficient for the abſolute perfection of theyr Goſpell to betraie euerie particular Ruler, and to worke treſon againſt euery king in his owne Realme: to fil vp the meaſure of theyr malice & wickednes they became Traitors againſt the Pope, the Emperour, the Biſhops al at ones, and fynallie without any reſpecte dydde violate and ſet at nought the Mageſtie and eſtate of all Spirituall and Temporall Rulers aſſembled together in the laſte Generall Councell at Trent. They were not aſhamed to raile at that moſte highe and honorable aſſemble of Chriſtendome (the only name whereof ſhould haue made them tremble, whoſe only becke all Chriſten men, euer ſythens Chriſten Religion begonne, reuerenced and followed) at Chriſtes higheſte Uycar on earthe, at all the Reuerend Fathers, the Biſhops and men of God, & al the moſte high & excellent Chriſten

Princes

Princes (among whome were the renowmed Emperours, first Charles the fifth, then Ferdinande.) and at a word to call them all thecues.

At what time the Princes and temporall Rulers did set their heads together to appeare and set at concord the state of Christendome, and the Bishops did purpose and study earnestly to expound and declare the Articles of Religion y were in controuersy, when that most holy and high Parlement of al Christendom was called & assembled together in one place: these new Gospellish Reformers were warned and warranted vnder Publike assurance, to come thither, to tell their mindes, and then to departe safely without any harme or daunger. The general letters Patentes, the sufficient and lawfull safeconduct of the Pope and the generall Councel were written, Printed, and Proclaimed for their behalfe herein. No man appeareth, not one of them maketh any word or mention of Reformation there: the matter touching the Reformation of the Churche is disputed in the meane time, and debated amonge them

them in the campe, in the field, in battaile in Fraunce by force & might, by ſwordes & daggers, by gonnes and dubble Cannons.

And as for the Generall Councell, which was of purpoſe called to redreſſe and refourme all that was amiſſe, where the lawfull place, authority, and meanes of Refourmation was to be found, they paſſed not for it: they were called, and refuſed to come at it. They deſpiſed and cõtemned, they reſiſted and aſſaulted, they mocked and reuiled with moſte impudent ſcolding and railing that Generall benche and Court of all the Churche of Chriſte, that worthieſt and higheſt Conſiſtory of Chriſtendome. And the more to ſhewe their ſpite and deſperate malice, Montanus the Germaine, and Molinæus the Frenche man, and many other accompted no ſmall fooles amonge them, haue ſet forthe openlye in Printe in the name of all theſe Goſpellers their cankred, malitious, wicked, and diueliſhe defiance.

whome ſhall we accompte for frantike,

Moline.
Monta.
Apolo.
Eccl.
Angl.
& cæt.

like, madde, and furious men, but suche as are so farre beside them selues, so enraged, so Bedlemlike, that they knowe not men, they know no Law, no Magistrate, no common weale, no Church, no Religion, no God?

Ye haue hard (right learned audience) how these desperat and outragious castawaies and Rebels had no Authority at all to bid battaile, but conspired together like Theues, Cutthrotes and Traitors: may it please you now to be aduertised of that, which is by order the third and last part of my talke, that is, howe little furtherance, frute, or profit touching Refourmation, as they call it, they gotte by fighting, howe great and hurtfull losse, iniury, and damage they did therby to all the whole world, howe fearcely, cruelly, and Tyrannically they vsed themselues in handling their bloudy weapons.

And in this poynt I assure you in good faith I wot not what I may, nor what I may not saye, nor where to begin, so many and so manifold losses & harmes Christendome hath had euery waye, and

on

on euery ſide, by the occaſion of this wicked and cruell diſſenſion whiche began firſt wel nigh fifty yeares agoe in Saxonie about certaine Articles and queſtions concerning Religion: but ſithens y̆ time it hath bene maruelouſly ſpred abrode and enlarged, and is now come to this lamentable caſe, and tragicall ſtate as ye ſee.

It grieueth the very bottome of my harte to call to remembraunce howe vnluckely, how miſerably the worlde hath gone with vs, how pitifully the eſtate of Chriſtendome hath fallen to wracke, ſythens the firſt beginning of theſe diſmold and deadly diſcordes and battailes ſet a broche and ſtirred at the firſt vnder pretenſe and coloure of Religion.

I can ſcarſe abſtaine from wepinge teares, when I remember and conſider ſo ruefull, heauy, and lamentable a caſe. And as for the blowes, the woundes, the ſmart, theſe Butchers beſtowed on mens bodies: or the continuaunce of time may eaſe them, or the diligence of cunning men may heale them, or the charitable patiēce

of

of Chꝛiftian hartes may foꝛget them.
But that they haue banished the Chꝛiſtian Faith and Religion out of ſo manye
Realmes, that they haue with deceit and
craft, with fire and Swoꝛd, beaten and
dꝛiuen away all Iuſtice, Chaſtity, Deuotion, all good learning & good nurture,
all feare of God almighty, all goodneſſe
and godlineſſe from the hartes & mindes
of ſo many thouſandes Chꝛiſten men,
that they haue rooted vp the Religion of
Chꝛiſt, and planted in the ſteede thereof,
the Turkiſh Sect of Machomet, the ſu-
perſtitious doctrine of the Iewes, oꝛ rather ẙ Heathenniſh & vnſenſible blind-
neſſe of thoſe ẙ beleue in no God at all,
in many countreis that were ſometimes
the moſte floꝛiſhing and nobleſt quarters
of Chꝛiſtendome: theſe Iſay, theſe vntol-
lerable hurtes and damages are ſuche, as
neither may be amended eaſely, noꝛ reſto-
red quickly, noꝛ euer be aboliſhed & put
out of mennes remembꝛance hereafter.

They haue bꝛought vs in ſtede of Religion innumerable erroꝛs and dꝛeames,
accurſed Sectes of old doting heretiks,
and

and monſtruous phanſies of wicked and
diueliſh braines: their chiefe purpoſe and
intent was quite to ouerthrow the Eccle
ſiaſticall order of the Spiritualty, and to
bring the temporall eſtate of the Empire
and royall power of Princes to ruine &
decay. They were not aſhamed moſt impudently to ſay it. They were not afraid
moſt deſperatly to attempt it. what was
he that was wont whiles he was yet a-
liue to rehearſe this verſe, and to ſaye it
ſhould be the Epitaph of his graue?

Pomerā
reporteth
this of
Luther
in oratio
ne fune.
in exe-
quiisLu.

Thy foe, O Pope, I was aliue,
My Death thy Death ſhall eke contriue.

Hoſtis
eram vi-
uus, mo-
riens tua
mors
ero Papa

who was ſo impudent to wryte to the
king of England and ſay: whiles I lyue
I wil be the Popes enemy, and when I
die, I wilbe his dubble enemy. Do what
ye can ye Doggiſhe Thomiſtes, ye ſhall
finde Luther a Beare in your waye, a
Rampinge Lioneſſe in your walkinge
pathe.

Luth. li.
contr.
Re. Ang.

And touching their doinges, who is
able to expreſſe in wordes, what coſt and
charges, what paines and trauayles,
what anguiſh and care of minde the noble Emperour Charles the fift was put
vnto

vnto, by the occasion of these Pestilent Sectes and outragious seditions? How many Cities? How many Fortresses and Castels? How many Abbeis? How many Hospitals for poore people? How many common Scholes and Colleges? How manye honorable Palaices and Gentlemens houses? Howe many Religiouse places and Cloisters hathe this Gospellishe Rebellion quite ouertourned and sacked?

These mennes Religion is altogether Negatiue and denying: they denye in word all thinges that appertain to Christian religion, to the furtherance of godlinesse and vertue.

It is allso destructiue, and euer destroying: their deedes are alwayes employed in castynge downe and ouerthrowing. They builde nothing, they affirme nothing: the denying and marring of our Religion, is the foundation and making of their Sects. The sacking and pulling downe of our Churches, is the building and setting vp of their Synagoges.

They

They haue their purpose, if they deny all and pul downe all, though they build nothing, though they affirme nothing in place thereof. Their Religion wer made though they taught nothing, if all Chriſtian Faith were baniſhed. Their Temples were ready builded, if all our Churches were downe, though they layed neuer a ſtone.

The mortal enemy of al Chriſten men the Turke, by furtherance & help of theſe tumults, hath gotten Hungary, no ſmal portion of Chriſtendome: hath killed the king there & many a thouſand of his mē with him. I paſſe ouer with ſilence Alba Regia, and that noble Iſle of Rhodes, which wer loſt alſo by the ſame occaſion: yea and now we might haue ſure hope to recouer the Rhodes, Hungary, I may ſay Conſtantinople, & wel nigh al Grece again, to ye Chriſtian Empire, if the mater might be valiātly purſued after the great fal & foil our enimy had of late at Malta: but the rebellion & ſedition of theſe heretical ſectes doth let vs from this ſo Noble a victory, and doth as it were depriue Chriſtendome once agayne of all theſe
domi-

dominions and countreis.

I may boldlie saie it, ŷ these domesti-call bickerings emong our selues about matters of Religion, and insurrections of seditiouse subiectes that doe pretend Refourmation, are the onlie staie, hinde-rance, and let that standeth betwene vs ⁊ conquering the Turke.

what shal I talke of Schole dooies shutte vp, of Vniuersities (and namelie this Noble Vniuersitie of Louain, the nurcerie of al good learning) cōtemned, despised ⁊ called, stables of asses, stewes, and Scholes of the diuelles? what shall I saye of the solitarie nakednues, bare walles, ⁊ lacke of studentes at this time in those Vniuersities, ŷ before this re-fourmatiō attēpted, wer much frequēted, flouishing and most notable for learning?

A man may now scarse see a hundied, students of law at Orleans, in steed of manie hundieds that were wont to be seen there in ŷ quiet time of ŷ Catholike Churche. Angiers, Poictiers, Bourgys, Tolouse, worthy Cities whiche heretofore haue bene allwayes moste Noble nurceries of law, are now so naked ⁊ d

Luth. 75 propo. contra Loua-nien, & de abrog miss. priuat.

while were the Scholes in Oxford suffred to go down and the ordinarie disputations in Logicke and Philosophie left of in King Edward his dayes? Answer. D. Cox. Vide Coclæū de Act. Luth. 1524. A preacher in master Iewels diocesse sayed it openlie at a visitation, when he could not

bare, ẏ they haue but a Reater or two, and fewer scholers to heare, then were wont to be in a Grammar schole of the countreie, before this new Gospell was set abroche, and this grosse maner of Reformation with bowes, billes, & gunes attempted: & yet these impudent striālls are nothing a shamed thereof. It is theyr doinge, it was theyr meaning: they graūt it, they reioyce at it, theyr ful purpose & intent is to bannish al good learning and knowledge. Yea they haue set theyr heddes together and fully agreed among themselues, to bannish the Greeke & Latine tong quite & cleane out of the countreie.

And some of them accompted earnest setters out of the Gospell and taken among them for most eloquēt preachers, affirmed, that they were verie gladde, and thanked God highelie, that they had neuer learned that Romishe and Papistical Latin tong, as they called it: other, after they had done the best they could to pull vp all good learning by the roote, and hadde euerie where robbed, disturbed, and distroyed the Scholes,

Peda

Pedagogies and Universities, to excuse the whole matter, they bore men in hand, that they hadde comprised and framed the whole corps and Treasure of al good learning and knowledge within the compasse of theyr owne mother tong. They toke vppon them to bring to passe, that now a yong Scholer of fiften yeares of age might easylie in three yeares space learne more, come to better and surer knowledge, and proue a greater clerke and better learned, then euer his forefathers coulde in times paste with al theyr paines, trauaile, and studie, daie and night, fortie yeares together.

answer being asked what case was Decenter.

Luth. de erigend. Schol. ad Senat. Germ.

Luther caused the Cannon law to be burned openlie in Wittenberge. Carolostadius the Archedeacon of ye towne, and the very firste maried Prieste that euer appeared in the face of the world in our dayes, caused all Philosophie bokes, all Historiographers and Cronicles, all Logike bokes, all good Authors of humanitie, Grammar and Rhetorike that could be sownd there, to be set afyre and burned. In deed Luther was not there then preſent, he was in his Pathmos ſolitarie making his fifte Goſpell, oʒ his ſecond & new Reuelatious : & when he came home, he was verie muche offended w̃ the Archedeacon foʒ it, and ſaied that by ſuche meanes the Papiſtes onelie would be learned, and Proteſtants ſhould haue no knowledge noʒ learninge, to anſwere and reſiſte them.

Would God, theſe hariſhe peoples Bedlem madnes had bene ſatiſſied with burning of bokes only, had ſtaied there, had gone no further. Theyʒ raging furie proceded yet foʒward, euen to the burning of Chʒiſtẽ men, to cut their thʒotes, to hew, to mangle, to teare & chop them in peeries. Read ouer from the begining to the ending y̓ Cronicles and Hiſtoʒies of all the blouddie Tyʒannes that euer were, weighe and conſider all the moſt cruell & vnmercifull actes that euer anie Heretthes oʒ barbarouſe people committed, lay before your eies all y̓ tragical ſables, and hoʒrible fictions of Poeres: & yet ye ſhall plainlie ſee, that this Goſpell warre, this terrible fire and flame of conten-

tensiouse Sectes & Scismes, which hath
worne Christendom: and made it pyne &
decay well nigh now fiftie yeares, this
barbarouse Cruelty of these Gospellers,
this rude, fearce, vnnatural, & vnspeake-
able tyrannie of the Protestantes of our
time farre surmounteth, passeth & exceedeth
them all.

There were neuer found nor hard of
among anie wild & barbarouse people,
among bwte beastes, beares, Tygres
Lions, among the diuelles of hel themselues, suche vnmercifull, suche wonderfull examples of crueltie and bloudie
butcherie, as were shewed commonlie &
verie ryfe in these our vnluckie dayes,
sithens the light of this Gospell was
kendled firste with fire & gunpowder.

How saiest thou, Beza, I speake now
to thee, that wast not onelie presente and
priuie, but a cheife doer, & a moste cruel
Captaine in all these late treasons and
conspiracies that were deuised and attempted to suppresse & vndo Fraunce.
Tell me, I praye thee, when thou diddest commonlie goe vp to the pulpite in
Orleans with thy sword by thy syde, and

Beza es
Indiecie.

B iij   thy

At Orleans reported this Goſpell, of his to the Author.

thy Piſtolet (not S . Paules Epiſtles, nor S. Ihons Goſpel)in thy hand, diddeſt commonlie goe vp to the pulpite in Orleans and exhorted the people , that they ſhould rather ſhew theyr manhod & wreake theyr anger againſte ỹ Papiſtes who were the liue images of God , then againſte the dead and harmeleſſe images of ſtockes and ſtones that ſtood in the Churches : when thou diddeſt traine in and bring vppon that Realme all maner of miſchiefe : when hou diddeſt murder the Magiſtrates and Rulers, ſell tounes and Cities, make hauoke of thine owne natiue countreie, and geue the ſpoile and ſacking therof for a praye to forayners and ſtraingers : when thou diddeſt pull down and ouerthrow the temples and Churches of God and all his Saincts, and all auncient Monumentes of holie men of God : what Traytor what Tyranne , what Lion, what Satan could then be equall matche , or be compared to thee in falſehodde, crueltie , rage and wickednes?

Chriſtes holie will and pleaſure was , that his Churche ſhould be the place

place of prayer, and of his heauenlie
and Diuine Mysteries , not a den of Matt. 31.
theenes, not a brothell howse for hoores
and queanes , not an armarie for ar=
tillarie and weapon , not a couer or
camp for souldiours and men of warre.
But thou neuer camest within Chur=
che or Chappell , during all that tu=
multuouse trouble , whiche thou coul=
dest fynde in thye harte to leaue whole
and standing , whiche thou diddest not
desile and pollute with thy bawdie
pleasures , with thie mischeuouse vil=
lanie , with thie impiouse Sacriledge,
whiche thou diddest not at last robbe
rifle , spoile , rase , mangle , marre,
suppresse , pull downe and quite ouer=
turne.

  In deed thou haddest learned that
leasson long a go of thy master John
Caluine the Ringleader of al mischief,
who when he was a yonge man and
Student in law at Orleans , being
chosen , as the fasshion is there , by
his contremen y students of Picardie, to
be y Proctor of his nation among them,
and had , according to the custome , the
                  S ii y Chalice,

Schole fellowes in law reported this of him to the Author.

Chalice, the Crosse, the Uestimentes and all the Churche oznamentes that appertained to that worshipfull companie of his countremen, committed to his charge, custodie and credit, to keepe for their vse and for the celebration of Gods seruice on highe feastes, and at their Ordinarie assembles, and solemne dayes of Meting : the false theefe toke his heeles and ranne away with al, offended God, robbed ý Churche, & deceaued his own contremen that trusted him so muche: thereby euen presently to geue al Christendome an euident signe and token of the great Sacriledge that he committed afterward in Christes Churche, and a lesson and paterne for thee to follow.

When in Champaine, thou tokest manie honest vertuouse and learned Priestes prisonners, and diddest keepe them as captiues taken by the law of armes, promising them their liues for their ransome, & yet afterward because they and the people there would not agree & consent to thie wicked doctrine, diuelish heresies, and furiouse raging dreames

dreames, diddest syt vppon them like a
Bedlem and cruel iudge, and condemnest
some of them to prisonnes & dungeons,
some to be hanged, some to be burned,
other to be beheaded, pronouncing most
wrongfull and vnmercifull sentence of
death vppon them: when this impudent
face and wicked mouth then talking and
preaching diuelishe doctrine, was in the
meane time sparkled & sprinckled with y
blond and braine of those that were put
to death and murdred at this foote, what
sprite possessed and ruled thee then? what
crumme of reason? what sparkel of pitie?
of mercie? of mans nature haddest thou
then lefte in thy harte or bodie?

How manie vertuouse men & honest
Priestes were slayen and murdred after
most cruell maner in that insurrection,
by thy deuise and counsel, by thy persua=
sion, procuring and compulsion, by thyn
own blouddie and butcherelic handes &
weapons?

At Orleans a good old man, called
Guiset, parson of S. Paterns Churche
there, and an Abbote also, one that was
somtime of the Frenche kings counsel,

        G v   two

Theſe things ar notoriouſlie knowen at Oꝛleans.

two Notable pillers and ſhining bꝛight examples of true Chꝛiſtian Religion and vertue were put to death and hanged vp on a galowes, that is yet to be ſeen in ẏ market place of that Citie.

An other old Religiouſe man nighe foure ſcoꝛe yeares of age of the Abbey of S. Euuerte there, when he had eſcaped out of Oꝛleans, and gotten a mile oꝛ twa from the Citie, was taken by the ſouldiours of the Goſpell in a certaine Uillage called Marrau, where he had receaued his maker that moꝛning pꝛeparing himſelf to die, ⁊ out of hād they ſtrip him ſtarke naked, and caſte a rope with a riding knot about his necke, and ſo pulled him ⁊ dꝛew him a long the ſtreate. when they ſaw he was now at deaths dooꝛe, ⁊ geuing ouer ſtruggling gaſped foꝛ bꝛeath they toke awaye death from him leaſte it ſhould eaſe him to ſone of his paine, they vntied and looſed ẏ coꝛde, they toke his feble and now wel nighe dead carcaſſe, bownd hit to a tree, and made hit theyꝛ marke to ſhoote at with theyꝛ harquebuzes and gunnes, foꝛ exerciſe ſake and pꝛactiſe of theyꝛ featies of warre.

A ij

An others bealy they opened, & wounde out his guttes about a ftaffe softe and faire, he being yet aliue and looking on his own entrayles.

They came to an other good parson of a Village in the countree who laye sore sick in his bedde, so worne & spente with sicknes, that for very weaknes he was not able to ftã on his fete. They plucke him out of his bedde by force, they hale him in his sherte bare headed, barefoote and barelegd out into the streate. & after they had sported and mocked like mad men about him a while, they pull him in to ye Churche ye was there hard by, they hoyfe him with a rope vp to the roode that ftode a highe ouer the quiere doore, and there hanged him vp vppon the crucifix.

I haue yet fresh in my remembrance, yea my thinke I see yet now before my eies the teares of certaine honeft men in Orleans, who for weeping & snobbing could scante abide to tell me, how miserably how cruellie, how vnmercifully a certaine vertueuse mã a Prieft, withe whome they had been familiars

and

and acquainted in his life time) was handeled & murdred by these cruel butchers. The poore houest man (as they told me) got on a beggers cloke, and a scripp full of crustes of old vinowed bread, & scraps of meate such as beggars haue, & being so disguysed had escaped, as he thought, out of all gunneshot and danger, when behold, sodenlie Caluines souldiours ouertake him on the waye being now weerie and nighe out of breath. And, as these kind of people are verie suspiciouse, wel practized and experte in al mischiefe, they aske and examine him verie diligentlie, what he was, and whence he came. when by long examination and muche threatning they vnderstood at length y he was a Priestc, they brought the innocent poore man bound like a theef into the next Village, and there in the open market they make an auction and sale of him, as if he had bene a bondman, and aske, if anie man would geue readie mony for him.

The inhabitāts there flocked together & were marueiloustie amased & astonied at so strange a case, they beginne to intreate

treate for him, they praye them, and holding vp theyr handes to heauen they beseeche them hartelye, that they would dimisse & let goe the innocent & harmelesse man, and doe him no more harme: that they would consider, that he was a Christian man, the image of God and anoynted priest. But it had been as good they had told a tale to a tubbe, or whispered in a deaf mans eare. For all Heretikes haue stonie hartes, they can not be mollified. It is the nature and propertie of men, and not of diuelles, to be moued with mercie and pitie towardes suche, as are in miserie.

To be shorte, first they pull out both his eies, then they cut of ỹ toppes of his fingers whiche had been sometimes anoynted with holie oyle, and flea with a knife the skynne of ỹ crowne of his head whiche was shauen (according to the ancient Custome & Cannons) Priestlike. After they had thus mangled hym, to the end the cruell butchers of the Gospell might haue some more pastime in mockinge and laughing at him, they leade him along the streat stark naked, sauing
that

that he had a poore ſhurte on, to couer his black, blew and blouddie bodie, and diſioynted bones that were bruſed and wel nigh all cruſſhed wᵗ buffets blowes and woundes. At laſt when euerie man had his fyll of this vnmercifull, cruell, and raging mad paſtime, they binde the conſtant Martyr of Chriſte, with a rope vpright againſte a tree, and with theyr gunnes ſhot at him ſo often, that they perced all his bodye thzoughe full of holes.

O God immortall, that thou ſeeſt theſe ſo wonderfull and ſtrainge villanies, ſo horrible and incredible cruelties, and doeſt not out of hand ſtrike down & conſume awaye Suche monſtruouſe men with fire and lightening from heauen, oz cauſe the earth to open and ſodenlie ſwalowe them aliue down headlong into the bottomeleſſe pit of hel? O lord God moſt mightie and omnipotent King and Emperour of al heauen and earth, ſuffreſt thou thy ſeruants to be thus diſmembzed, hewed, and mangled?

But what talke I wretched, earthlye and

and mortall man so foolishlie after the maner of man with the euerlasting, immortall, and almightie God, my lord and maker?

It seemed beste so to thy eternall wisedom, O mercifull God, it stood so with thy heauenly will & pleasure, that the might and power of vs thy seruantes the Christians, shoulde be made perfit by weakenes and infirmitie, that such as fought manfully, as they should doe vnder thy banner, should be rewarded w a heauenly croune, & be honoured with an immortall garland of triumphe and victorie, that thou wouldest bring vs throughe fire and water into a place of reste and comfort, that suche as would leese theyr liues for thy sake, should be reuiued and restored into life euerlasting. The onely euerlasting, and immortal sonne of God our Captaine lord and Emperour Iesus Christ taught vs firste of all by his own example and Passion to treade this path, Sithens the first houre that the crosse was halowed, adourned, and decked w his sacred & blessed bodie as with a moft pretioufe and celeftiall Margarite. His diuine prouidence made the Croffe & all affliction in this world light and eafie to true Chriftian men, his example and imitiation hath made al tribulation and aduerfitie pleafante and fweete.

This was ᵽ cheife reward that our Mafter Chrifte gaue in this world to his deare difciples, the noble Princes and worthy Prelates of his Church, to al the moft vertuoufe, holy and good men in al ages, that they fhould take pleafure & be glad, ᵽ they were accompted worthie to fuffer reproche & miuries for his names fake, that they fhoulde willinglye and gladlie take vp theyr Croffe on theyr fhoulders and follow him theyr mafter & guyde that lead them the waye.

It is not therefore, O happie foules, it is not fhame for you, to fuffer ᵽ Chrifte fuffred: nor glorie for thefe bloudie traytters, to doe that Iudas did. To him that winneth, Manna is geuen and a white Stone, and a new name which no man knoweth, but he ᵽ receaueth it. Ye haue wonne the field, ye liue, ye raigne like
Kings

Apoc. 2.

Kinges and Emperours. O ye happie and moste valiant souldiours of Christe. For this wages and for such recompense we are contented gladly and pleased to suffer and abide the cruell tormentes and butchery both of the Diuel him selfe, and also at the handes of these his Garde & wayting yeomen, his membres and most wicked Ministers of hel.

O ye cruell Tyrans, Gospelspillers, and Messengers of all naughtie and wicked tydinges, goe on and fill vp the measure of your cruelty, and impietie. Ye labor in vaine against ye seruantes of God. they are yet aliue, whome ye haue slaien. They had the vpper hande ouer you, whom you thought ye had ouerthrowen, oppressed and vanquyshed.

They raigne and rule, whome you contemned, despised, and trod vnder your feete.

The pitie & compassion of this cruell acte hath lead me further then I thought, out of my waye. But whyther was I minded to trauaile being alreadie weary? I labor in vaine if I trauaile to recken vp all the vilanouse deedes, ye wonderful

F i mur-

murders, ỹ cruel tiranny of theſe naughty villaines. The reherſall of all the Tyrannicall and barbarous actes of theſe new Reſourmers in this laſt ſedition in France, were able to make a good Diator weary, yea to driue out of breath Fabius himſelfe, were he neuer ſo well diſpoſed to talke. And I perceiue (right worſhipful and learned,) that it goeth againſt your ſtomakes to heare theſe horrible doingtes, and in very deede it goeth againſt my hart alſo to ſpeake ſuch thinges as the Goſpellers and Proteſtantes of our daies do put in practiſe gladly, & with all their heartes.

They thirſt after bloud, and can neuer haue their fill of it, nor quench their thirſt with it. They would faine that all good men were rid out of the way and deade. nor they thinke it ſufficient to haue them all dead: they wold wiſh they died a hundred times, if it were poſſible for a deade man to reuiue and liue againe a hundred times. They inuent and deuiſe incredible faſhions and meanes of cruelty, ſuche as neuer man hard of before, they are very witty and expert in imagining newe
kindes

kindes of tormentes.

There was betwene Paris and Orleaus an honest man a Curate of a certaine village: this man the Hugonotes (as they call them) drew in by force & might against his will into their Inne, where they lodged. when they had him there, the most wicked butchers first cut of his priuie members, then they open his bely, he being yet then aliue and loking on, and with their bloudy hands pull out his guttes and all his bowels, and caste his entrailes about all the house.

If any man suspect that I faine, and imagine of my owne head this wonderful cruel deede, and lie vpon them: I am able to bring for witnesse of this butchery y I tell you, a substantiall man both honest & worshipfull, one of the Prebendaries of the goodlye Cathedrall Churche of S. Crosse in Orleans. This man, (whome I woulde here name to his worshippe, if I coulde call his name to my remembraunce) all the while this vile and cruell murder was a doing, laye hid in that house shut vp in a cheast or benche, and so escaped these Tyrannes cruel handes,

D. ij.   and

& ſaw this ſorowfull & lamentable ſighe through the chinks of the benche where in he laie.

But what neede I bringe any witneſſe for the profe of ſuch things as are notori ouſe and manifeſte, as being committed in the preſence and ſight of al the country? Our aduerſaries are not aſhamed to cō feſſe it them ſelues, they rubbe theyr for heddes, caſte awaie all ſhame and ho neſtie, and bluſſhe not a whit to graunt that they haue done ſuch things in deede, yea they laugh, and ieſte, & make a moc king game of it, & do reioyce & triumph in theyr wicked crueltie. And ſome of thē at theyr death (and God wil) do comforte them ſelues eſpecially with ſuch deedes of mercie and workes of charitie.

There was one of theſe Butchers at Paris the laſte yeare condemned to be hanged for murder in the market place called Place Maubert, and when the hal ter was about his neck, he beganne to reioyce in good earneſte, and to brag that ſometymes he had worne about his neck a coler made of prieſts eares. and wiſſhed that other of his brethren in the Lorde
would

would followe that notable example of his: and because that, dying in so high degree he had no authoritie by the lawe to make his testament, this exhortation and counsel stoode in steed of his laste will & testament.

They broke and burned the crosse, and mocked at it euerie where as the Turkes did sometyme at Constantinople, neither were they satisfied with that: they toke two innocent good Priestes and hanged them vpon eche side of the Crucifix like the two theeues for contempt & reproche. Other had theyr faces and fingers flcied, theyr noses, eares, and priuie members cut of, theyr heades clouen with a sword at one stroke in two partes. Some they burned aliue, and yet moste commonly they are wonte to pull vp the dead out of theyr graues, yea and they toke maruelouse delight & pleasure to cut litle children and babes in two at one stroke with a sword. And these were the straingé and wonderfull miracles that these Posles wrought at S. Macaries.

Now what they did to a notable vertuose old man, a Religiouse Prieste at

An. 1452.
Vide Du bitantiú Lindani. pag. 198.

D iij   Mans

Mans the chiefe Citie of Cenomania in Fraunce, I am afraid, yea I tremble and quake to rehearse. That horrible Act don emong Chriſtian men hath defamed and blemiſhed the name, not only of all Chriſtians, but allſo of Heathens, Turkes, and all mankinde.

Many excellent & graue wryters haue put in wryting manye a time and often, that there be in ſome partes of the worlb Anthropophagi, that is, ſuche people as do eate mannes fleſh. But that any wold compell a man to eate and ſwalow down the priuy partes of his owne body, being cut of and broyled on a grediern, and thē would open his bealy being yet aliue to ſee if mannes ſtomake could brooke, concocte and digeſt ſuche ſtrange kinde of meat, ſuch men hauing the face and likeneſſe of men, that would attempt and cōmit ſuch a dede ſo ſtrange, ſo abhominable, ſo diueliſh wer neuer yet foūd or hard of before theſe our daies of Reformation. Such a deteſtable & brutiſh acte was neuer done or practiſed amōg any deſperate & wild people, among barbarous & rude natiōs, amōg moſt fierce and cruell brute

beaſtes

Du ſacc. fo. 72.

beasts before this our vnhapy time. And what was ẙ cause (I pray you) of this so cruel & strainge punishment? what had this mā offeded? what was his trespasse?

In the old time he that had killed his own father shuld be sowed vp in a lethern bag, and a dog, an adder, a cocke, and an Ape win the bag with him: and being so beset and accompanied with those vgly, dismold and deadly mates packed about him, was cast aliue into the sea, if it were nigh, els into the next riuer. So ẙ being yet aliue he lost the vse and seruice of al ẙ foure elements at ones, the aier, the fire, she earth, ẙ water, because he had bereued that man of his life, by whose benifite he was brought to the world, and to the vse of all these.

And this strainge kind of most shame= ful & ignominious punishment & death, was executed only vpon those ẙ had kil= led their parēts, for their vnnatural, vile and abhominable offense. But this mā, ẙ was put to so strainge, filthy, & infamous kind of most cruel death, who was cōpel= led against nature to eat his owne flesh, which euery man spareth and cherisheth, shuld haue

Institut.
de pub.
iudi
ẙ aliat,

haue bene of likelihood giltie of ſuch, ſo
great, ſo vilanouſe a treſpace, that excepte
he had bene rydde out of the waye and
put to the moſt cruell death that coulde
be inuented, the whole frame of all the
world muſt nedes haue fallen downe and
peryſſhed. And yet to this miſerable
man, who ſhalbe ſpoken of hereafter to ỹ
worldes end, and be pernouentuce the
rufull argument and lamentable matter
of tragicall ſtages, this only faulte was
laied, that he was a Chriſtian man, a Catholike, a Prieſt.

It was againſte theyr will that ỹ Miniſters of the Goſpell puniſhed him ſo
cruelly, but yet for Reformations ſake
they could not chuſe but of neceſſity do it.

For reformations ſake alſo I doubt not
(as the Reformed brethren in Chriſt doe
fondly beleue) they ſacked, ſpoiled & threw
doune to the grounde the moſt Chriſtian
Kings houſe at Orleans, and the goodly
Temple of S. Anian that ſtoode by it
buylded with Princely worke of ỹ kings
charges, and al the faire and riche Churches of that noble and renoumed Citie,
excepte certaine litle Churches whiche
they

The Au-
thor of
this orati
on hath
ſeen all
theſe
ruines.

they fpared to put in their Harneſſe, Artillary and prouiſion for warre, and the chiefe Cathedrall Churche S. Croſſe, which they reſerued ſtanding (but yet all to rifled, raſed and mangled) to preach in and to be the place of their dailye walke for recreation.

The Engliſhe men, who by the lawe of armes, by manhode, princely proweſſe and force of warre had conquered and wonne well nigh all Fraunce, could neuer ouercome and get the ſtrong, mighty, and moſt defenſed walles and rampiers of Orleans. But this Goſpelliſh Reformation in this laſt Inſurrection in Fraunce, hath filled vp the Ditches with earth, ſtones, and rubbell, hath throwen downe to the ground, the ſureſt towres, the ſtrongeſt Bulwarkes, all the defenſe of the Towne, and all the ſtronge holdes and Fortreſſes round about, they haue made the walles ſo flat and plaine, that in ſundry places Cartes and Horſes may eaſly paſſe ouer, yea they haue brought al the goodly ſtreates, Suburbes & Vines about the Towne to a bare, barein, and naked field.

The

The moste Christian king Lewys the eleuenth his body was buried Honorably and princely, in a goodly tumbe richly garnished, with his Image grauen on the outside, in our Lady Church at Clery, foure leagues from Orleans. For reformations sake they did hew the kinges Image in peeces, cut of his armes, feete and head: and when they thoughte they had sufficienly punished the Image, they open the sumptuous & honorable graue, pluck vp the kinges body out of the lead wherein it was enclosed, caste it into the fire and burne it, and at laste they spoyle the goodly Church that was trimly builded with costly and faire worke, they vncouered the toppe of it, and caste it quite downe.

Claud. d Sainctes fol. 70.

For Reformations sake the harte of good king Francis the second (who died lately poysoned, as it is thought, by the meanes of these Gospellers,) that was buried before the highe Aultare in the Churche of S. Crosse at Orleans, was digged out of the ground, broyled on a grediern, and at last burned.

For Reformatiōs sake, Orleās, Roan, Lions,

Lions, and many other rich Townes in Fraunce, the whiche florished sometime with great traficke of marchaundise, are brought to extreame pouertye and miserable lacke and scarcitie of all things necessary. And haue fewer occupiers, porer Marchauntes, and are lesse haunted, then euer they were before in any mannes remembraunce.

How many parents bereaued of their children, how many children benummed of their Parentes, how many widowes weping for the death of their husbads, how many Burgiscs turned out of house and home, are nowe to be sene commonlie in Fraunce latelye reformed, and all for reformations sake?

S. Peter had neither golde nor siluer, Act.3. nor yet passed vpō the getting of any: he gaue to the pore man that asked his almes, helth in stede of money. But these newe Postles the disciples of Iudas Iscarioth and Simon Magus, who trauail toth ē nail not to alter & change, but to abolishe and take quite and cleane away both law and Priesthode, haue exceadinge greate

store

ſtore of gold and ſyluer which they ſcraped and gathered together by robbinge and ſpoiling and ſacrilegiouſe ſacking of Churches, and yet they geue neither money, nor helth to ſuch as aſk their almes: they feede them with faire wordes, and geue them ſometymes ſtripes, blowes, wondes and moſt cruell death in ſteed of almes.

They ſay that the Cleargie is to riche, and therefore they take away both from them, and from the laictie alſo without reſpect or partialitie, ſuch hindrance letles & impedimentes of pietie, deuotion, and perfection : And they them ſelues in the meane tyme, good men, doe beare patiently vpon their neckes the ſynnes of the people, and al this traiſh & mucke and heauie burdens. They throw down townes and Cities, ouerthrow Temples and Churches, to get gold, without the which theyr Goſpell can not be planted, the world can not be reſourmed, yea they go into y bowelles and bottome of the earthe. They robbe the dead to fill theyr owne purſes, they open and breake vp ſepulchres and graues to haue y very
lead

lead wherein dead mens bodies, bones
and asshes are wrapped.

what tounge is able to expresse in
wordes the spoile, saccage and ruines,
of the Churches of Poictiers, Lions, and
of other townes in al quarters of France?
This is moste certaine, that Beza and
his companions, Theenes & cutthrotes
like him selfe, stole out of the Churches
and Vesteries at Tours two thousand
markes in syluer, and a thousand marke
in gold, besides pretiouse stones, chaines
and other Jewels, and ornamentes of
greate valew, yea and that with suche a
rage, such an vnmeasurable desyre and
outragiouse couetousnes, such a furiouse
affection and thyrste of stealing and hauinge, that they scratched all that euer
they could by anie meanes, and lefre not
as much as a naile or peece of yron be-
hinde them.

And bysydes all this, the Holy Beza
dubbled this myscheuous robbery of his
with an other enormous outrage, so
haynouse and greate, that no condigne
and worthy ponisshment can make sufficient amendes for it. For he toke away
the

the ſacred Relyques of the bleſſed Archebyſſhoppe of Tours, the body and aſſhes of S. Martyne the Greate Confeſſor, that had bene kepte there, with greate reuerence ſo many hundred yeres, notwithſtandinge the often warre and cruell perſecutions of diuerſe enemies both heathen and Chriſtian. And when he had taken them out of the Shrine, he burnte them with fyere, and then gathered vp the holy and bleſſed aſſhes, and threwe them into the Ryuer of Loyer that runneth thereby.

With the lyke impietye and ſhameleſe rage at Lyons the bodie of S. Irenens ſometyme Byſſhoppe there, one that liued very nigh the Apoſtles tyme: at Poictiers the bodie of S. Hylarie Byſſhoppe alſo there, were pulled out of theyr Graues, defiled, Prophaned, burnte with fyre, and then caſte into the Riuers.

O wonderfull Impietye and madnes of raginge Heretikes, O beaſtly and more then Barbarouſe rudenes and crueltie. What Tyranne euer in anye Lande was ſo fierce and cruell, that would

---

marginal notes:

Diuus Martinus Epiſ. Turonenſ. floruit An. Do. 384. Tempo. S Amb. & Chry. & cæt.

S. Irenæ. Epiſ. Lugdu. claruit. An. 185. S. Hilar. Epiſ. Pictaui. claruit. An. 361

woulde perfecute , teare and mangle all good men, not only in theyr lyfe tyme, but also after they were departed out of thys world, and buried in theyr graues? These cruell Graueroorers, that labor to brynge a newe Religion into Chriftendome, can not abyde, that good men fhoulde lyue any where on the earth, nor yet fuffer them to reafte vnder the earth in theyr graues after theyr deceafe.

They couer with Sylke, and decke with veluettes theyr owne fylthye bodies , and theyr womens mofte vple and ftynkinge carcaffes, whiche (without the greate mercy of God) fhallbe one daye the ftuffe and matter of Hel fyre, and carrayne for death and damnation to feede on: And wyll they not fuffer the blelfed bodies and bones of Sayntes, that fhallbe in the end placed in Heauen with theyr blefled foules, (whiche are there before in peace, and reaft, and ioye with Chrifte) to be in the meane tyme clofed in lead, or coueted with ftone, or layed vnder earth and claye?

It is

It is happy, they can not plucke theyꝛ holy Soules out of heauen to, as they doe al theyꝛ endeuoꝛ to deſtroy and vtterly rydde theyꝛ bodies out of the earth. Foꝛ if they could gette them thence, & ſet themſelues in theyꝛ places, it appereth here by this good wil of theirs in ẏ one, what they would doe in the other: and that is no moꝛe, but euen to follow their Grand Capitaine Lucifer. Foꝛ as he would haue done to God himſelf, when he ſayed in his harte, he would clyme aboue al ẏ ſtarres of God, and be Gots owne fellowe and ſyt faſte by his ſyde: euen ſo by al likelihod, theſe men would doe to Gods fryndes and ſeruantes. that is, robbe them of all gloꝛy, and of theyꝛ places both in heauen & earth, if it lay in theyꝛ power ſo to doe. But though God geue them alitle leaue on theyꝛ bodies whiche is all that they, oꝛ the the diuell hath any power vpon (Foꝛ the Serpent feedeth on the earth and crepeth on his belie, and can do no moꝛe)yet Sanctorum Animæ in manu Dei ſunt, & nõ tanger illos tormentum malitiæ. The Soules of Saintes are in Gods owne hand, and reaſt

Gen.3.

Sap.3.

teaft and raigne with him, that all the malice of ý diuelles in hell, oz theyz ſeruantes in earth cannot once touche, noz tome nere them, what euer they doe in the meane tyme to theyz bodies.

I cannot let paſſe, but rehearſe and note here vnto you ſurely a notable Hyſtorie out of Euſebius, of the perſecutiōs of the very ſelf ſame places in Fraunce: by which it may be thought in cōſerring the one with the other, that theſe men nowe be of the ſame feruēt and hot zeale (as themſelues terme it) of the ſame mynde & opinion in theſe lyke actes of theyzs, as ý curſed Paynyms were then toward the Chriſten folke, whome they perſequuted and put moſt cruelly to death. For they, not content with all the terrible tourmentes, paynfull deathes & Martyzdomes executed vpon them, would not ſomuch as ſuffer theyz bodies to be buried, but threw them to dogges, and kept ſtraight watche day and night, ý noman ſhould take them away, but that ý dogges ſhould deuoure them in deede. And if the beaſtes, oz the fyze leafte any part of theyz bodies not conſumed

Euſeb. Cæſ. Ec. Hiſt. lib. 5. Cap. 3, le Martyr. apud Viennam & Lugaum.

I

famed, they toke the bones and aſſhes, and the duſte, and all together, & threwe into ye Riuer: thinking thereby to ouercome and conquere God himſelfe, that neyther he ſhoulde be able to gather theyr aſſhes together, and make theyr bodies aliue againe, as they were before: nor they haue any hope of Reſurrection, out of theyr graues, being out of all hope of graue, or any kynd of buriall at all.

Circiter An. 166. in qua perſecutione paſsi ſunt Irenæus, Photinus, Blādina &c.

This doth Euſebius wryte & reporte out of the very lettres and Autentyke wytteneſſe of the Chriſten folke & Martyrs there at that tyme. And if we ſhal côpare together thoſe myſcreantes then, with theſe our myſſeſhapen Chriſtians nowe, I cannot ſee wherein they any thing differ from them: but well may I ſone ſee, that in ſome pointes theſe matche them, & go beyonde them to. For the perſons and holy Sayntes of God, againſt whome all this crueltie and extremitie of malice is ſhewed, be all one, of the ſame Catholike fayth and Religion, and much about the ſame age and tyme, far within ſyxe hundred yeres after Chriſte. And what els is the cauſe, that

that our newe Gospellers doo so persecute, spette at, and abhorre theyr bones
and ashes nowe, but for the hate they
haue both to them and theyr Catholique
Religion, if they durst so playnly for
shame cōfesse it, as by ye diuelies persuasion they doo in theyr hartes beleue it.

The Paynyms would not only themselues not burie the dead bodies of the
Sayntes, but dyd also most cruelly forbyd, and most straightly watche, that
none other mā, nor Christen nor heathen
moued with pitie, should steale them a-
way and burie them. what els meane
these Captaine Protestants nowe, but ye
neyther they, nor any good Christē man
in deede, shall see any such holy bodies
reuerently buried and layed in graue?

The heathen Infidelles cruelly kylled
the Christians, as theyr mortal enemies,
and threwe theyr bodies to beastes to de-
noure: These worse than Infidelles take
vp the bodies that haue so long lyen styl,
spoyle the graues and Sepulchres, and
prophane all together most impiously.

The Infidelles, to wreake theyr present āger, forbyd burial to their enemies,

I ij being

being newly ſlayen , theyr blood yet warme, and the tormentors wrath yet freſſh and fierce : theſe fell perſecutors denie them buriall , yea moſt violently ſpoyle them of theyr graues, which they had quietly kepte and poſſeſſed ſo many hundred yeares. whome if they take for theyr fryndes, why order they ſo cruelly: and if for theyr enemies , why haue they not forgot all yre and malice after ſo lóg tyme of ſo many hundred yeares?

Twelue hundred yeres and aboue.

The myſbeleuing Paynyms thoughe, that the Chriſten men ran wyllingly to ſuffer all kynde of torment and death for Chriſtes ſake , becauſe of the hope they had to lyue and ryſe againe , and enioy a better lyfe & crowne of euerlaſting glorie. And that therefore they deſyred ſo muche to be honeſtly buried , that theyr fleſh and bodies might lye together, and ſo the more eaſyly be reyſed vp and made againe by the power of God. And to the end , that God might not come by theyr fleſh, and ſynowes, and bones , nor they haue any hope at all of Reſurrection, and thereby alſo be dryuen from theyr conſtant and patient ſuffring for Chriſtes ſake:

ſake: they ſought the meanes not only
not to burie them , but alſo that God
ſhould not any where fynde and come by
theyr fleſh and bones , & aſſhes againe:
but toke all , and gaue it to beaſtes to
deuoure, and to the fyre to conſume . and
then what the beaſtes & fyre had leaſte,
they threw earth and aſſhes and al toge-
gether into the Riuer , to be vtterly diſ-
perſed , and neuer to be recouered and
got together againe.

whether Beza & his fellowes in theyr
like dede of burning the Reliques and
holy bodies of Sayntes , and throwing
theyr bones and aſſhes into the Riuer,
haue alſo the lyke mynde and opinion of
Gods power and Reſurrection: J committe to the ſecrete iudgement of God,
who moſt certaynly both ſeeth theyr
thoughtes, and the moſt priuie corners &
ſecretes of theyr hartes , and ſhall reyſe
vp his holy Sayntes & Martyrs bodies
to immortal lyfe and glory, where euer y
cruell Jnfidell , or impiouſe Heretike
ſcatter and flyng them abrode in y wyde
world.

But in the meane tyme well may we,

J iij   (as

(as Chriſten men dyd then in thoſe greaſ perſecutions, when they could by no meanes be ſuffred to bury ẏ dead bodies) lament to ſee & heare of this Heathen & Myſcreant maner, this moꝛe then Tur-kyſh crueltie of ſuche, as would be not only counted true Chriſtiãs, but alſo pꝛe-tend & ſtoutly take vpon them to be Re-fourmers of the Catholike fayth. wel may we rue, and be ſoꝛy to ſee this daye. well maye I nowe and woꝛthely crye out, and make exclamation: O moſt mercyfull loꝛd, O euerlaſting God of heauen and earth: what a wycked and Barbarous Religion, oꝛ rather Ir-religion, what a ſtrange and rude Re-foꝛmation, oꝛ rather Deſoꝛmation is this, that purſueth with famine, fyꝛe and ſwoꝛde all good men, euery where, and allwayes, yea, after they are de-parted this lyfe? that encreaſeth, ga-thereth foꝛce, and is ſtrengthened with turmoyling and troubling all Commo weales and good Oꝛder, with robbing & ſpoylinge theyꝛ owne contreemen and neighboures, with contemning and pꝛo-
phaning

phaning all holie and Spirituall things,
with breaking vp and violating of Se=
pulchres, Schrines, and Graues, with
kylling & murdering all faythfull Sub=
iectes, with dasshing and huddeling all
the affayres & good orders of the whole
worlde together, w blasphemies, mad=
nes, furie, rage, crueltie, butcherie far
passing the Turkes Tyrannie?

What els shall we coniecture & deeme
to haue been the marke and end, intente
and pourposes of suche Refourmers as
these be, if it were not to abolishe & roote
out quite all Christian Religion out of
the worlde? they haue omitted no kinde of
crueltie that could be deuised, they haue
slayne and murdred the honorable and
worshippull, the substantiall and ver=
tuouse subiectes, they haue spared noe
state, nor age.   The rage and furor
of these sauage & Barbarouse wretches
hath extended it self and waxen fearce
and cruell againste children, women and
old men : who were so weak, that they
were not able nor to hurte other, nor
yet to defend and saue themselues.

A iij   There

This cruel dede was don in a Village called Patte not far from Orleans.

There was a companie of honeſt mēs Children, who for feare of theſe mad-braines paſſing by, ranne to hyde them-ſelues into a Churche, the villaines did ſet a fire and burned both the Churche, & the chyldren together, and when ſome of ꝑ poore infantes lept out of ꝑ fire to ſaue their liues, theſe cruel broilers & vnmer-ciful murders far exceding the tyrannie of the wicked Herode flong the ſeelie in-nocentes aliue into the fire againe. They had no care, nor regard at all of honeſtie, ſhame or chaſtitie. They ſtripped an ho-neſt mayed ſtark naked as euer ſhe was borne, in the middes of the ſtreate at Or-leans. And when ſhe ſtood ſo, openlie a-mong them, ꝑ bawdie ribaudes Sarda-napalus ſouldiours feeled and groped her ſhamefullye, filthylie, and againſte all the lawes of nature, to ſerche forſooth if ſhe had hidden anie money, aboue the rate of the proclamation, to carie priuilie out of the town about her.

The traytor by Angiers which kept a caſtle againſte his Souueraigne lord and maſter the King, and toke a Noble wo-man and hāged her in a baſket by a rope
over

ouer the Castle wall for a bullwarke against þ force & shotte of the Kings artillarie and battering pieces, did suerlie a more cruell and vnmercifull acte: but yet not so durtie, filthye and bawdie, as this fowle deed which nature abhorreth.

Theyr full purrpose and intent was, to pille, robbe and spoile all they could get, & to leaue nothing vntouched. Gabastone the master of þ watche or rather the master of misserule at Paris seemed plainlie to confesse and proteste, that this was their mening, at what time he was in the companie of these Sacrilegiouse Refourmers at the spoiling of S. Medardes Churche there in the firste beginning of the trouble, and rode on his horse into the quiere before the highe Aulter, and there gabbled and cried to his mates in his barbarouse Gascoigne Frenche, Pilla tout, Pilla tout, that is, spoile all, spoile all.

Is there anie thing I pray you, more fearce, more cruell, more horrible, that men should need to feare at the Turkes handes, if he had been in place, then that we haue seen, to our greate greife, smarte

J v   and

and dammage, attempted and committed by these vile Pages, and Pedlers of
this newe Gospell? Truelie I beleue
Soliman ý great Turke himself would
neuer haue suffred Virgines and professed Nunnes to be so filthylie deflonred
and forced by rape, the Priestes and seruantes of God to be so villanouslye and
spitefullye handeled, all holye thinges
consecrate to Gods seruice and honoure
to be so wickedlie defiled and profaned,
finallie the verie blessed and pretiouse
bodie of our lord and master Christe him
self to be with suche furiouse and outragiouse impietie, caste on the grownd,
trod vnder foote, hurled into the fire
and into the water, and so desperatlie to
be prickt with theyr swerdes, and caried
vppon the toppes of theyr speares.

Uerylie thus I thinke, and thus my
mynd geues me (right worshipfull and
learned) that except that onelye Noble
man, the right honorable Duke of Gnyse
had withstood theyr furiouse attempts,
and defeated theyr moste cruel assaultes
and desperate enterprises, that most Noble parte of Christendome the whole
                                   comon

common weale and Realme of France had been vtterlie vndone and loste. And that notable vertuouse man, a personne moste famouse for passing manhod, exceading vertue, & peerlesse knowledge & commendacion for warfarre & feates of armes, the father & defender of his countreye, the glasse & bright shining light of al France whiles he went about to quenche the flame, to parte y strife, to appeace y sedition of his contreie, was traiterouslie & cruellie murdred by the meanes, counsel and vnmercifull conspiracie of that vile Caytif Beza, the inuenter & coyner of al these michiefes, & seruante & bondslaue of al bawdie luste, fylthie concupiscence, and all detestable sinne and vice.

See the confession of Pultro the murderer.

I feare me leaste I seeme to passe y limites & compasse of y time apointed for me to speake by y custome of this Schole, & to abuse your gentel patience & suffrance (right worshipfull) if I trauaille anie further with longer discourse & to long talk, to declare & rippe vp y endlesse and infinite desperatnes crueltie, & madnes of these harishe Ministers, traiterouse Reformers and brutishe Heretikes.

To

To be ſhorte, your wiſdomes I doubt not doe plainlie now perceaue, that this theyr warre for Religion againſte God and all true Religion, hath been made, nother iuſtelie, nother orderlie, nother to anie good effect or furtherance of Reſourmation. Ye ſee now as clere as the bright ſhining ſonne, that the Proteſtātes of our time ranne raiſſhelie together and toke weapon in-hand without anie iuſte cauſe, reaſonable occaſion, or ſufficient quarell: that they badde and proclaimed warre againſte theyr counntrey, againſt cheyr Soueraignes, againſte y Catholike Churche of Chriſte without anie commiſſion, power or Authoritie: y they foughte that battaille to fearcelie, to vnmercifullie, and to cruellie, to the exceeding great iniurie, harme and wrong of all good men, to the incredible hindrance, and dammage of all Chriſtendome, and ſuche loſſe as can neuer be repayred. Ye know now theſe new Goſpellers, the wicked Captaines of theſe moſte traiterouſe and dangerouſe inſurrections, ye vnderſtand what maner of men they be, how vprightlye, how honeſtlie

nestlie they liue and behaue themselues
in the Churche of God, and what they
meane, what they go about, what they
attempt.

what saye you, then by them? what
punisshement, thinke you, haue suche
bloudsuckers, suche cruell butchers deserued to suffer? what estimation, what
degree, what state among Churka men
iudge you suche verlets to be worthy of,
whome neither shame could withdraw
from dishonestie, neither feare keepe of
frome danger, nother reason renoke from
madnes, nor Religion stop from Sacriledge, nor pitie staie from killing and
murdering of theyr own neighbours?

At the firste for a messe of potage certaine loose friers and fained dissemblers
of Monasticall profession fell out at debate betwene themselues, & afterward,
they were pricked, dryuen and drawen
by auarice, ambition, and wanton luste
of wicked libertie and pleasure to strike
vp a larme and to bid battaille: and at
length they fought in open field against
theyr own contremen, neighbours, and
fellowes, againste y̆ Magistrates, Kings
and

and Emperours, againſt the Biſhops, againſte the Churche, againſte the Chriſtian Religion, againſte all good men, againſt the Sayntes of heauen, & finally againſte God allmightie himſelf, as the Gyãtes did, of whome ẙ Poetes in theyr ſables make mention, meaning in deed ſuch deſperat, raging & wicked caytiffes, rebelles & miſcreants, as theſe were.

The falſe traitors & deſperat cutthrotes brought into the Churche of Chriſte a curſed kind of Religion, framed, caſte, & made of wicked whoredomes, & bawdie bitcherie, of innocent bloud and murder of true ſubiectes, of all maner of troubleſome and ſeditious miſchiefe & diſcord, and all looſenes and libertie to embrace and follow vice & ſinne. They haue called in, holpen, & maintained the enemies of Chriſtendome, Forayners, Tyrans & Turkes.

They haue geuen to the Turke and added to his dominion and Empire manie Noble and goodlie countreies & prouincies of Chriſtendome. They haue lead an infinite nũber of Chriſten ſoules

to eternall damnation , throwen them
down hedlong to the deepe pit of euerlasting fire , and betaken them to the tyrannie and furie , of the vglie findes and
horrible diuelles of hell.

They made the holie fonte stones
the couers of theyr iakes: yea the durtie
Helhowndes (Oh abhominable acte)
were not ashamed to laye the excre-
mentes of theyr vile and wicked bealies
euen in the verie sacred fonte and place
where Christen men were wonte to receaue theyr Baptisme.

There were slayen in Germanie within three monethes space by the wicked
occasion and faulte of these Reformers
an hundred and thirtie thousande men,
and in Fraunce aboue a hundred thousand , among whome I recken not the
infinite number of suche as died of the
plague there in y meane time, of whome
the greatest parte were these Cutthrotes
themselues , speciallie they of Lyons ,
who , as it is reported , did poison the
welles & common waters of theyr Citie for a traiterouse and wicked intent:

So that by the iuste iudgement of God it is brought to passe, that there scars remaineth now aliue vppon the earthe y fourthe parte of those, who for a great number being but beardlesse yong men and moste of them witlesse , & altogether desperat and destitute of y feare of God, attempted to doe suche , so strainge and villainouse deedes.

I will not staie now to make an accompte and iuste reckening of al those that throughe this cursed Refourmatiō were caried to miserable captinitie vnder the Turke, or were slayen in the field in defense of Christendome againste him and these his adherents : and yet this I am bold to saie, that if ye hard the euen tale & iuste accompte of them , ye wold more wonder at it & pitie it , then ye doe now at the rehearsall of this marueilouse nūber slayen and murdred in Fraunce and Germanie.

They haue turned all lawes out of y countrey , and sent all right and equitie into bannishement. deuotion, true Religion, Chaste lyuing can wel nighe now abyde safe in no place : the Profession of
Chastitie

Chastitie is suspected, hated and despised euerie where. Al things are besette, and turmoyled with madnes, rage, murder, fire and sword The desperate crie of furiouse heretikes doth make all the world ring, the streates runne of bloud, the walles of Chapelles and Churches are sprinkled & dawbed with the gore blood and braine of Christen men: Al Europe, being weakened with the cruel warre & long seditions of heretikes, cracks, and shakes and is euen now readie to fall quite to the ground.

And now when al this is done, after al these mischeifs and Tragical offenses, ye these mad Bedlems, & cursed Caines haue committed: they blame the Catholiks and lay crueltie to theyr charge, that haue suffred all these iniuries, losses, damages, and murders at theyr haudes. There came furth in printe of late to the sight of the world a verie fond foolishe & peuyshe litle boke out of Englande, writen againste the tyrannie of the Papistes: for so it liketh them in scorne to call the Catholikes.

In these and suche like dangers often-
B   multes

multes and inſurrections of ſubiectes, (right learned Audience) in theſe verie ſame ſnares and trappes of treaſon and cōſpiracie we alſo ourſelues haue liued & ſtood nowe a long time. we nouriſh in our owne lappes & boſoms Domeſticall enemies: who raging with deſperat boldneſſe, and panting for verie malice, doe imagine & labor to poiſon & vndoe theyr Countrie, & breake out into ſuche common talke & dailie communicatiōs, as abode add threaten the murder of all good men, and the ſetting of the Citie a fire. This cruel, this horrible, this contagiouſe and deadlie plague, we haue by the benefite & mercie of God allmightie, and the diligent prouiſion of graue and wiſe Rulers often times eſcaped.

If it were writen in euerie mans forehead what he thought of the Common weale, ye might reade murder, blond, & burnings, the bane, wherling gulphes, and ouerthwart rockes, prepared to poiſon, to ſwalow vp, to ouerthrowe ỹ Citie at home within your own houſes, abrode in the Churches, in the Scholes, yea & ſometimes in this verie auditorie where ye ſtand.   Learne

Learne by other mens dangers, lasse & harme, what hangeth ouer your owne headdes, what is like to fall on your Citie, your Churches and aulters, what is like to become of your lines, your goods and substance: if (whiche God forbyd) this your countrey also should happen to be sette a fire with this terrible flams of discord and Rebellion.

There is no hope of forgeuenes, no looking for mercie, no place left for pardon, where the rage of these Gospellers beginnes to get ye vpper hãd, or theyr desperat furie to beare the swaie and rule. Nother the regard of their Countreie, nor of parentes, nor wiues, children, nor frendes shalbe able anie whit to moue or mollifie the hard stonie and more then Adamante hartes of Protestãtes. They will not set a russhe by the weeping, wayling, and teares of theyr frendes & acquaintance, they will caste away all feare, and set naught by the loue & frendship both of God and man, and breake as muche as euer they may all God and mans lawes, and moste desperatlie cutte the throte of euerie Christen man thy

B ij   meete

meete, when they perceaue ẏ they haue
the ſtronger ſyde.

Tread out therfoze and quenche the
ſparkles of this fire now whiles ye may.
Doe not winke anie longer at theſe mõ
ſtres to your own ſmarte ⁊ harme. Do
not nouriſſhe ⁊ cheriſhe in your howſen
and by your fire ſyde theſe venemouſe
Eſopicall adders to your own vndoing
eſpeciallie, and to the deſtruction of all
good men.

Ye haue heard, what they haue don
other where: you vnderſtãd therby what
you your ſelues alſo ought to feare. Foz
whiche of you al, oz what honeſt man in
all the wozld wil they ſpare, think you,
who are ſo malitiouſe ⁊ ſpiteful againſte
all good men, that they can not find in
theyz hartes, to let them reſte in theyz
graues, noz pardon them when they are
dead and buried?

There is no honeſt man, yea no Chzi=
ſten man (who at leſte remembzeth him=
ſelf to be a Chziſtian) that can abide to
ſee ſuche villaines, ſuche Goſpellers,
bontchers, traitozs, madmen, wicked
Church robbers, that can abide to heare
of

of them : whose harte riseth not against them, and finallie detesteth and abhorreth not theyr crueltie, and tremoleth not at the verie remembrance of theyr Tyrannie.

*E Go Frater Ioannes Hentenius sacræ Theolo-
gia professor Louan. præsentibus mea manu
scriptis attestor, prædictam orationem in lingua
primûm Latina editam, mea approbatione, nunc
autem in linguam Britannicam versam nihil
continere, propter quod minus in luce edi debeat,
imò plurimum vtilitatis ad fidem Catholicam
tuendam allaturam aduersus hareticos. Hoc
autem quoad versionem hanc idcirco audeo at-
testari, quanquàm hoc idioma non calleam, quòd
id certò mihi asserant Docti ac Catholici viri
Anglicanæ Nationis.*

IO. HENTENIVS.

THE TABLE OF
THIS BOOKE SET OVT
not by order of Alphabete or nūbre,
but by expresse figure, to the eye & sight
of the Christian Reader, and of
him also ȳ cannot reade.

B iiij.

The first note & storie in this litle booke
to skan,
The Gosplers in Paris streates thus in
a rage ran,
with Gospel in their mou. hes & swozde
in their handes:
I see not how these two together well
standes.

B vii.

Calnin in his chamber fiue yeres taught
  a Nonne
Tyll she was great with Gospell and
  swolne with a sonne.

C i.

Beza solde to two men his lininges of
  the Churche,
And ran his way with all, and left them in
  the lurche.

His white Mystresse Candida a taylors
    wyfe before,
Of her charite for al Christen soules
    fetcht one schisol more.

Caluin bannisht Fraunce, Geneua did
    possesse,
And all the lawful Magistrates did expel
    and oppresse.

Rotman for the Lutherans draue the Ca=
    tholikes out,
  John Leid for the Anabaptists, expeld the
    Lutheran rout.

Muntzer with his Gospellers & vplandish
    bande,
  The Princes & Magistrates doth stoutly
    withstande.

Mary Towne and Castel and Palaice
    of renoune.
Mary Churche and Chapell is quite
  throwen downe.

LVTER

The Turke against Christen, by Chri-
    sten is calde in,
With more then Turkishe treason and
    most horrible syn.

E. v.

The Emperour in warre is assayld o̧ eche side,

More perill in his life did he neuer abide.

GOODMAN   KNOKES

E. vi. F. ij.

No Queene in her kingdome can o̧ ought to spe fast,

If Knokes o̧ Goodmans bookes blowe any true blast.

E vi. F ij.

Many Kinges in their Thrones this
  Gospel did shake,
And made many mayne landes full
  terribly to quake.

CALVIN

F v.

The Chiefe of Christes Churche sitte
  in Councell to aduise:
Then al Prelates and Princes thinke
  ye yourselues more wyse?

B i.

Uniuersities, Colleges, and Scholes be
    ouertu. ned,
These men spette at Learning, they will
    haue al bookes burned.

B ii.

Beholde a good preachor, with a pistolle
    in his hande:
Against such pistle or Gospell it is to hot
    to stande.

A piſtolet in the Pulpit: what is the
   Churche then?
A ſtorehouſe for your weapon, and a
   ſtewes for your wemen.

CALVIN

Caluin beynge younge, the Croſſe and
   Chalice ſtale,
Beinge olde he did put greater th.ng3
   in his male.

B. v.

Upon poore priestes Beza in iudgement
    doth sitte,
Him selfe to be iudged and hanged vp
    more sitte.

B. v.

An Abbot and a Prieste at Orleans with=
    out pitie,
They hangd vp in the open Market
    place of the Citie.

A Religiouse olde man escaped with
   care,
They tooke againe, and stript him all
   naked and bare,
With a rope about his necke along they
   him drewe,
Bounde him to a tree, and with handgons
   him flewe.

             L

G vi.

An others bely was cutte, and his guttes
    taken out,
And wounde softe and fayre on a staffe
    rounde about.

G vi.

One out of his bed they pulde lying sore
    sycke,
And in the Churche, on the Roode they
    hangd him vp quicke.

An other that was fled like a beggar priui-
   lye,
They tooke, and stript, and set to sale with
   open outcry.
They flea his fingers & crowne, and pull out
   both his eyes,
And kill him with their hand gons, for their
   warlike exercise.

               L ii

And other at their bayt into their Inne they
   drewe,
  Ript his bely, and his guttes all about the
   house threwe,

Many Priestes had this man by like
  maymed and slayne,
Sith he coulde of their eares make himselfe such a chayne.

Two Priestes thus they hanged by the
  Roode for theyr game:
With Christ so to hange doo they thinke
  it a shame?

Some had theyꝛ crownes and fingers pared
    ſkynne and all away,
Some theyꝛ noſes and eares cut of by the
    barde head.
Some their pꝛiuie members cutte of in moſt
    ſhamfull play,
Some burnt vp,ſome with a ſwerd at a
    ſtroke ſtriken dead.

H iij.

Litle children for theyr pastime, and triall of
   stronge arme,
At a blowe they cutte asundre, without any
   more harme.

I iiij.

And some, that ran away into a Churche,
   in theyr ire
They burnt vp Churche and all, leuinge
   none scape the fire.

Yet an other olde Priest they tooke most
    cruelly,
And cut of his membres most villanously,
And broyld them on the coles, and made
    him thereof eate,
And ript his belie to see, how he could di=
    gest such meate.

Kyng Lewys Tumbe and hearſe his
    Image coſtly wꝛought,
His graue they ſpoyld and bꝛake, and
    burned all to nought.

The holy Saintes and Martyrs
    That nowe in blysse rayne,
These men would pull downe
    And martyr onse againe.
Else why on theyr bodies
    And bones that here reste,
Doo they shewe so much malice,
    As ye see here expzeste?

For shame I both hyde from your eares, &
    your eyes,

Howe a mayd was abused in most shame=
    full wyse.

If Noe curst his sonne Cham for his shame=
    lesse acte,

More accurst shall these Chams be for their
    shamefull facte.

PILLA TOVT

I i.

One Traytor to saue his Forte from
   gonshot and ail,
A noble woman in a basket hangth out
   at the wall:

I i.

An other in the Churche ryding armed
   cryeth out
In his gabbling Gascoine Frenche,
  Pilla tout, pilla tout.

The sacred holy Hostes kept for our most
    reliefe,
Of Christes true bodie, O Lord with
    what mischiefe
These fellons so fell, so cursed and so vile,
Burne, stryck, cast on ground, and vnder
    feete defile.

I v.

O noble Duke thy noble Death
  Doth well require of right
An other maner style and prayse,
  Then we can well endite.
The more those Actes and Death of thine
  Deserues immortall fame,
The more those Traytors get themselues
  Thereby eternall shame.

The Conclusion and Somme of the
Table.

O Christ: If these the first frutes be
   This Gospell doth vs geue,
The same thy Gospell not to be
   Ful well we may beleue.
Thy Gospell is of tydinges good,
   Of loue and peace the sede:
This Gospell doth all tydinges yll,
   All stryf and bloudshed brede.

PSAL. 138.
Viri sanguinum declinate a me.

O ye bloudie men away from me.

ST. COLETTE
The Declarations and Ordinances
Made upon the Rule
of . . . S. Clare
1622

THE
DECLARATIONS
AND
ORDINANCES

made upon the Rule of
our holy Mother

S. CLARE.

Permiſſu Superiorum. 1622.

*HEERE BEGIN THE
Declarations , and Ordinances
made vpon the Rule of the Poore
Religious of S. Clare . First are
set downe two Letters making
mention of the Approbation , and
Confirmation of the sayd Declarations and Ordinances, written,
and sent by the Reuerend Father
in our Lord , Brother William
Cassall , Generall Minister of
the Order of the Friar-Minors .
Of which Letters, the one was
written only vnto his humble and
poore Daughter Sister Collet,
the first Religious woman of the
Reformation of the sayd Order of
S. Clare : The other in generall,*

A 2   *both*

both vnto her, & all the other Si-
sters of the sayd Religion. The te-
nour of the first is as followeth.

VENERABLE, and deuout
Daughter in God, health in
our Lord Iesus, who is the
true Spouse of virgins.] I haue receaued your letters & heard the relation of your Confessour, concerning the matter of the Confirmation and Approbation of the Statutes, which you haue sent, and
caused to be presented vnto me :
the which although they are very
fit, and conuenient for the true obseruance of your holy Rule;neuer-
theles at the first sight of thē, they
seemed to me to be in some sort
difficile: wherfore as I was(concer-

A 3   ning

ning this matter) somwhat perple-
xed & troubled, I recōmended the
affaire vnto our Lord Iesus Christ,
and vnto the merits of holy Saint
Antony of Padua, (vnto whome
I would to God I were worthy to
be deuout.) At length I was perswaded (as I doe verily belieue,
through the merits of the sayd glorious S. *Antony*) that the aforesaid
Statutes were especially sent from
God. Wherefore I determined
with my selfe, not only to confirme
them, but moreouer also to Institute, Declare, & Authorize them.
Thewhich we now send vnto you,
& vnto vour Daughters, instituted, declared, strengthned, & sea-
led with the Seale of the Order, togeather with the solemnities and
assurances appertaining to such an
A 3   affaire,

affaire, both through the Authority of our Office and the Generall
Chapter , as also through Papall
and Apostolicall Authority which
we vse in this behalfe : exhorting
and admonishing the said deuout
Daughters present & to come, that
they receaue the said Statutes with
great deuotion , & humbly & effe-
ctually dispose themselues perfectly to keep them ; knowing for certaine that by the obseruance of
them (through the merits of the
most glorious Father S. *Francis*, the
founder of their holy Rule, and of
the most worthy Virgin S. *Clare*,
the first Plante of that most fruit-
full field (to wit of the holy Religion) & most plentifully aboūding
in vertues) they shall obtaine the
plentifull reward of eternall life.

Vnto

Vnto which Daughters, and first vnto you, I recommend my selfe; beseeching you and thē to vouchsafe to pray to God for me most vnworthy. Giuen at Genèua the yeare of our Lord 14,4.the 28.day of September.

The Tenour of the second Letter, is as followeth.

BROTHER William Cassall, Generall of the Order of the Friar-Minors, and Maister in sacred Diuinity, vnto Sister *Colke* Religious in Iesus Christ, Foundresse of many Monasteries of the poore Dames of S. Clare Minorits, at this present time built & erected in the parts of France; & vnto the Abbesse, & all other Sisters of the said Monastery, and vnto all those

A 4 other

other Couents present & to come, which vnder this forme and manner of life, shall be built & erected. Health in our Lord Iesus Christ the true Spouse of Virgins.] How much the great merits of the Noble virgin and glorious Lady S. Clare vnder Blessed S. Francis, Father & teacher of all Pouerty and holines, haue meruailously increased ; and how those merits shine in the holy Church of God, and of the Spouse of Virgins our Lord Iesus Christ, doth not only appeare by the reward giuen vnto her in the Kingdome of Heauen, and by the holy degrees of the glorious Saints of Paradise, which do signify euerlasting rest; in which degrees, amongst the Prudent Virgins she is singulerly glorified & crowned :

but

but alſo in this preſent time it is
ioyfully declared, & made known
by the great praiſe and worthy re-
commendation which is made of
her in the ſaid Church of God, and
eſpecially by the multitude of deuout virgins & other notable perſons, who in the order of her holy
life and ſweet conuerſation, according to her example, in flying and
ieauing the perills of this miſerable
world, do goe & run vnto the ſure
and ſafe hauen of Religion: for
the which we ought the more to
giue thankes vnto God, by how
much we ſee at this preſent, humane nature to be more enclined
vnto euill; and that notwithſtanding through the diuine aſſiſtance,
this holy Profeſſion doth not ceaſe
alwaies to budde, & produce new

A 5   plants

plants, not estranged from the in-
stitution of the glorious Father S.
Francis, & the traces and pathes of
the glorious Mother S. Clare, who
desiring with admirable feruour,
that the Rule & forme of life to
them giuen by the same S. Francis,
and admirably obserued by their
glorious Mother S. Clare, should
be expounded and fortifyed with
Declarations, and necessary Constitutions, that they may truly
repute themselues imitatrices of so
holy a Mother, & participate of
her glorious merits; amongst whó,
when I see & consider your Sister
Collet before named, Religious,
& Daughter in Iesus Christ (after
the holy Lady) especiall Mother,
& of these present writings, which
are for the repose of their Consciences

ciences, and safety of their soules,
& also for the perpetuall strength
of their regular obseruations, to be
Patronesse & intercessour : We at
your iust request moued & prouoked through your & their humble
prayers, do by Apostolicall authority graunted to vs in this behalfe,
send vnto you, both Abbesses & Sisters of Monasteries, by the grace
of God & your meanes founded
vnder the Rule & profession before named, & vnto all the Sisters
of the other Monasteries, which in
time to come shall be founded in
the forme & manner aboue mentioned, these present Declarations,
Statutes, & Ordinances to be perpetually kept: hauing maturely &
with great deliberation bin made,
& composed, & now authorized,

as

as aboue said, by Apoſtolicall authority, & likewiſe by our Office,
& the generall Chapter. Which declarations and Ordinances, are ſo
much the more by you to be eſtee-
med, feruently kept & obſerued;
by how much they haue bin more
diligently viewed, examined, and
notably approued by the moſt Reuerend Fathers in our Lord, the
Lord Cardinalls of holy Croſſe, &
of Saint Angell, Apoſtolicall Le-
gates, being actually preſent at the
holy Councell of Baſill, & by many other Doctours of diuinity; &
alſo by many venerable Fathers,
both for integrity of life & learning very famous: which Statutes
& Ordinances doe heere follow.

   First ſuch Daughters & Siſters in
Chriſt may doubt, whether by the

vow

vow they make at their Profeſſion, when they promiſe to keep the
forme of life which is their Rule,
they be bound by commaūdment
to obſerue the holy Ghoſpell, to
wit, as well the counſailes as the
commaundments: the cauſe which
may moue thē to doubt is, for that
in the ſaid forme of life there is
three times mētion made, To keep
the holy Goſpel: the firſt is cōtained
in the beginning of the forme of
life which ſaith; The forme of life
of the Order of Poore ſiſters which
S. Francis hath inſtituted, is this:
To obſerue the holy Ghoſpell of
our Lord Ieſus Chriſt, liuing in
Obedience, without Propriety, &
in Chaſtity. The ſecond is, where
it ſaith: You haue eſpouſed your
ſelues vnto the holy Ghoſt, choo-
ſing

fing to liue according to the perfection of the holy Gnofpell. The
third is at the end, where it faith:
Let vs perpetually obferue the holy Gofpell which we haue firmely
vowed. Vnto which doubt and
caufe thereof, we defiring to prouide for the confciences of the faid
Sifters, and take from them all difficulties which they may haue, in
fo much as is poffible for vs to re-
moue and take from them; doe
anfvvere conformably vnto that
which hath bin anfwered by many
Popes, namely Pope Nicolas the
third, and Pope Clement the fifth,
vpon fuch like doubtes made by
the Friar-Minors vpon the fame
points in their Rule; to wit, that
the faid Sifters by the vow which
they make at their profeffion when
they

they promise to keep the forme of
life which is their Rule, are bound
to obserue the holy Ghospell, in
the same manner that our Lord
hath deliuered it ; to wit, all things
which in the Gospell are commanded, they ought to keep as Commaundments; & the other thinges
which are counsailed in the sayd
Gospell, they ought to keep as
Counsailes: & are bound also as
vnto obligatory Commaundmēts
vnto such Euangelicall counsailes
which are put in their forme of
life, vnder the word, or forme of
commaundment, eyther negatiue
or affirmatiue, or vnder words of
as much force. But vnto other coū-
sailes of the holy Gospell they are
not bound, but as other Christians
are (excepting only, that in respect
they

they haue willingly offered, and
giuen themselues to follow the example of our Lord Iesus Chrift,
through the contempt of al worldly thinges, their Profeffion requireth, that they tend vnto greater
perfe&ion then other Chriftians.)
Other thinges contayned in the
forme of life, as well commaundments as counfailes, & whatfoeuer
thing put in the fame, through the
Vow of their Profeffion, are not
otherwife obligatory, then as in the
fame forme of life is fpecifyed; to
wit, vnto Admonitions, as vnto
Admonitions, vnto Informations
as vnto Informations, vnto Exhortations as vnto Exhortations, &
vnto all other things they are boūd
in the fame forme & manner as is
there contained, & no otherwife.

Of

Of the Entry into this holy Religion.

CHAP. I.

ALTHOVGH that at the beginning of the second Chapter of the forme of life, it be contained, that the Abbeſſe may receaue any mayd for a Siſter, with the conſent of the greateſt part of the Siſters, hauing had before the licence of the Lord Cardinall Protectour of the Order; neuertheles, we conſidering the former eſtate of this Order as being in the beginning founded very neere vnto the Court of Rome, & to the ſaid Lord Cardinall, and being now ſo far of

B　　　　from

from the same; as also the strict pouerty of the said Sisters, & difficulsy which they should haue to send vnto the said Lord Cardinall, to obtaine the said licence : considering also that the iurisdiction and gouernement of the said Order, hath bin fully, and wholy committed vnto the generall Minister and Prouincials of the Order of the Friar-Minors by Pope Innocent she fourth, and many other Popes : we therfore declare & say, that the said Generall Minister through the whole Order, and the Prouinciall-Ministers in their Prouinces, and their Vicars, haue authority to giue licence vnto the Abbesse to receaue for Sisters, such as flying the world are foūd to be fit, obseruing she manner which is contained in the forme of life.   1, We

1. We ordaine that according to the Ordinance of Pope Innocent the fourth , when any shall present herselfe to vndertake this Religion (before she change her secular habit and receaue the habit of Religion) there shall be declared vnto her , the most hard and difficult points which are to be obserued in Religion , to the end that after her reception , she haue no occasion to excuse her selfe of ignorance : and none shall be admitted , who for age , sicknes , or foolish simplicity were not fully able to obserue this manner of life: for by such the state and vigour of Religion , is oftentimes destroyed,or slackned.

2. Further,we will & ordaine, that the Sisters obserue this manner in receauing any person vnto

the Order; to wit that when any is
to be receaued, they first send her
to some sufficient person out of the
Order, fearing God, and louing
the Poore, to the end by his counsaile her goods may be distributed
vnto the Poore: and that the Abbesse and all the Sisters take heed,
that neyther by themselues, nor
by others they do receaue any of
the goods of them who enter into
Religion, vnles it were so small a
matter, that those vvho should
know of it, could haue no occasion to iudge sinisterly against them,
or that she who entreth wold giue
something vnto them, as vnto o-
ther poore, in manner of almes, to
relieue their present, or neere-at-
hand necessityes, and this comming from her owne freewill; for
the

the forme of life doth require, that
those who enter be free, and doe
with their goods, as God shall in-
spire them.

3. The Abbesse and other Sisters shall also take heed, that for
the reception of any person, they
doe not permit others to doe by
them, or by others for them, or
for others, any couenant or paction,
on, in which might be noted any
spice of Simony : also they shall
not permit that those who enter do
reserue any of their goodes in the
world, but that they offer themselues wholy naked of all earthly
thinges, into the hands of our cru-
cifyed Lord : but if it should happen that any one could not so spee-
dily discharge, & rid herselfe of
her temporall goods, and that she
B 3   were

were no way content to returne a-
gaine vnto thofe thinges which fhe
had fo left; fhe fhall in the beft fort
that fhe can poffibly, commit the
faid goods in fome certaine manner, vnto fome perfons fearing
God, to diftribute the fame vnto
the poore.

4. To the end, that in time
to come the fifters proceed more
Regularly; we ordaine that none
be receaued vnto their forme of
life, vnles they plainly perceaue,
that fhe come vnto the Order principally for the loue of God, and
health of her foule; and that fhe
be not thereunto only moued by
the fleight motions, or through
perfuafions, conftraint, or feare
of any perfon; but of her owne
freewill, as being chiefely mooued
there-

thereunto by the inspiration of the
holy Ghost ; and that they take
great heed that none be receaued
into the Order, except she be of a
good will, and a faithfull Catholike ; that she be not touched with
any publike infamy ; and that she
be of vnderstanding, and of body
sound ; not suspected of any heresy ; discharged and freed of her
temporall goods ; not bound with
sentence of Excommunication or
Interdict : but if it should happen
that she were bound with the sayd
sentence, that she be duely absolued before her reception, by the
priuiledges heerupon graunted vnto the order of the Friar-Minors :
neuertheles that they giue her to
vnderstand, that if she returne a-
gaine to the world, she doth againe
　　　B 4　　　　　　　incurre

incurre the said sentence , and
shall be bound therewith as before.

5.   Item, that she be free,and
not of seruile condition , to wit , a
Prentise ; or if she be , that licence
of her Maister or Mistris be had; &
that she be twelue yeares old before she be cloathed with the habit
of Religion ; and none shalbe receaued vnto the Profession before
the 18. veare of her age ; for before
that time she cannot be able to sup-
port & vndergoe the burthen of
Religion .

6.   We ordaine also,that none
be receaued for the Quire after the
25.yeare of her age,except she were
so copetently learned that she could
learne to read the diuine office ,
without great labour or hindrance
                                vnto

vnto the others : alſo that none be
receaued vnto Profeſſion who cannot ſay by her ſelfe alone , or at
leaſt with others in common , the
diuine Office: & that they receaue
none vnto the Order , except it be
manifeſt , that ſhe haue liued honeſtly and well from the thirteenth
yeare of her age , vntill the ſayd
tyme of her reception into the
Cloiſter : & that none be receaued
after the age of 40. yeares, except
ſhe were ſo Noble that her reception might notably edify the ſecular
people , and Clergy ; or that ſhe
were ſo ingenious and moſt ſtrong
that ſh e were able to ſerue God, &
the order according to your eſtate
and forme of life .

7. Further that none profeſſed of
any other Order be receaued vnto

B 5   you

your forme of life without the licence of her Abbeſſe, or priuiledge
from the Apoſtolicall ſea.

8. In like manner we ordaine,
that if the profeſſion of any Nouice
ſhould be doubtfull before the end
of the yeare the Abbeſſe in the preſence of the Siſters ſhall make pro-
teſtatiõ vnto her, that although the
ſayd yeare ſhould paſſe, ſhe ſhall
haue no right in the Religion, vntill ſuch time as by mature deliberation they haue determined what
they ought to doe, eyther concerning her Profeſſion, or her returne
to the world.

9. When they receaue any vnto
Profeſſion, ſhe kneeling before the
the Abbeſſe ſhall ſay leaſurely with
a high cleare voice in this manner.

In

In Nomine Patris; & Filij : & Spiritus Sancti. Amen.

I Sister N. doe Vow vnto Almighty God; vnto the glorious virgin Mary; vnto our holy Father S. Francis; *vnto our holy Mother S.* Clare; *and vnto all the holy Saints; and vnto you Reuerend Mother*

*Mother Abbeße, and vn-
to all your fucceſſours fuc-
ceeding in your place; to
obſerue all the tyme of my
life, the Rule and forme of
life of the Poore Siſters of
S. Clare, which hath bin
giuen by S. Francis vnto
the ſayd Saint Clare, and
hath bin Confirmed by our
holy Father Pope Inno-
cent the Fourth, liuing in*

O B E-

*OBEDIENCE,
without PROPRIE-
TY, and in CHAS-
TITY, also obseruing
CLOISTER, accor-
ding to the Ordinance of
the sayd Rule.*

Then the Abbesse who doth
receaue her, doth promise vnto her
(if she do obserue that which she
hath vowed) the eternall life.

10. We also ordayne, that at
the Cloathing, the hayre be cut off
round, and aboue the eares, & that
after that tyme they doe neuer suf-

ſſer their hayre to grow **long** : but
that often in the yeare , by the appointment of the Abbeſſe , all the
Siſters alike haue their hayre cut ;
except that for ſome ſicknes or
weaknes it were thought conuenient to do otherwiſe .

Of the quality of their Habits, and
of their Garments.

CHAP. II.

VVHEREAS it is contai-
ned in the Rule , and
forme of life , that the
Siſters be cloathed with poore and
vile cloathes.

   1.   We ordayne , and determine, that this vility be vnderſtood
concer-

concerning the price & the colour,
and although that it be contayned
in the sayd forme of life of those
who enter into this Religion, that
the secular Habit being taken away
the Abbesse shall lend her three
coates and one cloake; neuertheles
if necessity, or sicknes, or the con-
ditiõ of the person, or of the place,
or of the tyme, should cause any
of them to haue neede of more
coates; we declare that the Abbesse
(vvith counsayle of the Discreet)
may duely prouide for those who
haue the said necessity, considering
that the sayd forme of life doth also say, that the Abbesse shall discreetly prouide her Sisters of
cloathes, according vnto the quality of the persons, of the places, of
the tymes, and of the cold regions,
like

like as she shall see it to be expedient vnto their necessityes.

2. It is to be vnderstood that
the three coates which are expre-
ssed in the forme of life, ought not
to be all of one forme and fashion;
for the two vnder-coates are graunted them, only for warmth and
for the decency of the body, nor is
there obligation or need they be all
of one colour.

3. Therfore we will and ordayne, that the vppermost coate be
called the habit of the Order, without which it is not lawfull for any
of the sisters to goe, or to be seene
in publike, or to sleep, vnles for
sicknes, weaknes, or other manifest
necessity it be othervvise iudged
expedient by the Abbesse or Vicaresse, with the cosent of the greatest
part

part of the difcreet .

4. The habit fhall not be fo lóg
that it traine on the ground vpon
the Sifter that weareth it; and in
largenes it fhall not paffe the mea-
fure of 14. palmes; the length of the
fleeues, fhal be but to the knockles
of the hands.

5. The vnder coates fhall be
of vile and courfe cloath, and fhall
not be doubled with furres. The
cloake alfo fhal be of vile & courfe
cloath, and fhall not be curioufly
gathered or pleighted about the
necke, nor fo long that it traine
on the ground: but alwaies in all
their garments fhall manifeftly appeare aufterity, vility, and Pouerty, both in the manner of making,
price, and colour; and in this fort
both the Abbeffe, and the fifters

C   in

in office, and all the other Sisters,
shall be cloathed vvith common
cloath without any partiality. The
corde with which the sisters girde
themselues shall be common, vile,
without any curiosity.

6. Furthermore we appoint
and ordaine, that all the sisters as
well the Abbesse as the other sisters
without any difference, couer their
heades in all humility, decency, &
Religiosity, without any curiosity,
or vanity : and to the end that this
be the better kept and obserued of
the sisters, & of all their Couents,
we orday ne that all the Sisters shall
in such sort put on their kerchers,
that their fore-head, cheekes, and
chinne may be for the most part
couered, in such sort that none may
euer see them in the full face ; as al-

ſo their kerchers, and their veyles ſhall be ſo large, and put on in ſuch ſort that their whole head, & their breaſt, & ſhoulders be for the moſt part couered.

7. Alſo, we will that all their veiles and kerchers be of courſe cloath, to the end that in them doe alwayes appeare the holy pouerty and auſterity of their Profeſſion.

8. Furthermore, we doe allow that euery Siſter (vvith the conſent of the Abbeſſe) may haue two blacke veyles, and white kerchers, to chaunge them, and keep themſelues alwayes cleane, & decent. And that the Siſters take great heed that they neuer haue any kercher pleighted or curiouſly folded, nor their veiles of ſilke, nor any other coſtly ſtuffe.

C 3   The

9.   No Nouice shall weare the
blacke veile , before she haue expresly made her profession,except
she were before professed in another Religion ; but shall weare the
white kercher decently put on,ac-
cording to the appointment of the
Abbesse , & as it hath byn alwayes
vnto this time accustomed .

10.   To the end our beddes be
like vnto that , on which he dyed,
who sayth, The foxes haue their
holes , and the birdes of the ayre
their nestes , but the Sonne of man
hath not vvhereupon to rest his
head ; and to be also more wake-
full and diligent to rise vnto Mattins , and to be conformable vnto
our holy Mother S.Clare, who oftentimes lay on the bare ground ,
or rather vnto Iesus Christ the holy

of

of Holies, who had no other bed then the sharp desert; we ordaine that no sister (if she be not sicke or very weak) do sleep otherwise then only vpon a sack filled with straw, with couenient couerlets according to the discretion of the Abbesse: but vvith the sicke the Abbesse ought charitably to dispence, as it is contained in the Rule and forme of life.

11. Further we ordayne, that according to the example of Iesus Christ, and the glorious virgin S. Clare, the sisters goe bare-foote in signe of Humility, Pouerty, and mortification of the sensuality, contenting themselues only with wodden pattens vnder their feete, hauing a list nailed aboue to hold thê on.

C 3   Of

Of the diuine Office.

CHAP. III.

CONCERNING the diuine Office which they muſt pay vnto God as well by day as by night , let this be obſerued; that before all the Canonicall houres , immediatly after the firſt peale is ronge, all the ſiſters ſhall come into the quire to prepare their harts for our Lord , except they were law-fully excuſed in ſome affaire which could not be deferred , and that according to the iudgment of the Abbeſſe or her Vicareſſe, and there they ſhall remaine without going or comming, or without laughing,

making

making noise, or vainly looking a-
bout, but perseuere all togeather
vvith one courage in peace, silence,
Religious grauity, and due reuerence.

2. That none presume to goe
forth of the Quire so long as the
diuine Office is a reading, except
they haue licence of the Abbesse, or
her Vicaresse, or of her who pre-
sents her place, vntill the whole
Office be accomplished.

3. We exhort all the Sisters in
our Lord Iesus Christ, that alwayes
& in all places they accomplish the
diuine office attenctiuely, distinctly,
entierly, and Religiously; and they
must begin and make their stops
togeather; they must also with one
and the like courage perseuere vnto the end, in such sort that the

C 4   great

great Office be alwaies said higher
and more leasurely then the office
of our Blessed Lady, and that of the
Dead.

4. Concerning the måner to ring
vnto Masse, as vnto the Canonicall
houres, and the manner of siting,
kneeling, rising vp, bowing and
standing tovvardes ech other, the
Sisters shall alwayes obserue the
custome of the Friar-Minors, except in some Ceremonies which
are not conuenient for them.

5. Furthermore no sister that can
reade (of what condition soeuer
she be) shall be excused from the
Quire, eyther by night or day, but
all the sisters are bound to come
vnto Masse, and vnto all the Canonicall houres, excepting those
who are sicke, or those who are

to ſerue them , vvith leaue of
the Abbeſſe or her Vicareſſe ,
and thoſe who in the time of
the Office ſhould be occupied in
ſome common ſeruice of the Couent , vvith the knovvledge and
leaue of the Abbeſſe : and therfore all the officers ought to haue
ſuch forecaſt in their affayres and
offices , that they diſpatch them in
ſuch ſort as they may accompliſh
the diuine office in the Quire with
the others .

6. The ſiſters alſo who cãnot read
and are not ſicke or imployed in
the ſeruice of the others, ſhall likewiſe come to the Quire to fulfil the
diuine office , vnto which they are
bound, and that in ſome place aſſigned vnto them : and if the Abbeſſe
or her Vicareſſe ſhould find any ſi-

ſter

ster negligēt in the aforsaid points,
they may duely punish her, according to the quality of the offence.

7.　Further we ordaine, that
on the two dayes betweene the
feast of S. Clare, and the Assump-
tion of our Blessed Lady, they shall
serue the feast of S. Clare with nine
Lessons ; the other dayes of the
Octaue after the said feast, they
shall make a commemoration of S.
Clare at *Benedictus*, and *Magnificat*:
the Octaue day being the feast of
S. *Ludouicus*, which is *Duplex ma-*
ius, they shall make a Comemora-
tion of S. Clare at both the Euen-
songs and Mattins.

8.　Againe we ordaine, that in the
time of a generall Interdict, the sisters conforme themselues vnto the
principall Church of the towne, or
place

place where they reside when the
said Interdict shall be lawfully sig-
nified vnto them, by those vnto
whome it appertaineth, or by their
certaine messengers or letters; and
then the gates of their Church being shut, and the excommunicated
being excluded, the sisters shall say
all the diuine office as they say the
Office of our B. Lady on simple
feasts, not sitting but standing, according to the custome: & if it should
happen, that within the time of the
said Interdict, any deputed to the
seruice of the Couent, or any of
the Sisters within should fall sicke,
they shall communicate them; & if
they should dye they shall be buried with a low voice, hauing in like
sort exciuded forth those who are
interdicted or excommunicated; so
neuer-

neuerthelesse, that nothing be o-
mitted appertaining to the Office
of the dead, or Communion.

9. And for as must as it is contained in the forme of life, that the
Sisters who can reade shall say the
Office of the dead, without expre-
ssing the day, houre, or by what
manner or obligation they shall
discharge it; such is the obscurity of
the letter, as also the diuersity of
opinions and writings vpon it, that
I cannot giue any certaine resoluti-
on how they shall performe it;
therfore to take away all ambigui-
ty and difficulty which may a-
rise in this point, to discharge their
Consciences, and the more to suc-
cour and relieue the poore soules
of the faithfull departed; I will &
ordayne, that hence forward be
done

done as we haue alwaies accustomed, to wit, that euery day all the
Sisters say the Office of the Dead
with one Nocturne and the Lau-
des, except the Thursday , Friday
and Saturday of the Holy Weeke,
& also when they reade the whole
Dirige of three Nocturnes. The sisters who cãnot read shal likwise e-
uery day say the Office of the Dead
with *Pater Nosters* , as is contained
in the forme of life .

10. And for as much as prayer
is necessary to goe torward in the
seruice of God and make progresse
in vertue , we ordaine that for this
effect there be deputed for euery
day two particuler houres , the
one after Mattins , and the other
after Euensong, with a quarter of
an houre after Complin , for an
exa-

examine of Confcience.

11.   Alſo to keepe the body
better ſubiect to the ſpirit, and in
remēbrance of the Paſſion, and eſpecially the moſt cruel flagellation
of our Bleſſed Sauiour; we like wiſe
ordaine that the Siſters take diſci-
pline, three a week in Aduēt & Lēt,
& two a week the reſt of the yeare:
which, with the aboue mentioned
point of prayer, we will ſtill haue
obſerued, vnles for ſome occaſion
it be for a time omitted, which is
left to the diſcretiō of the Abbeſſe :
but if it should be for any long
ſpace, she is bound to aske the
counſell of the Diſcreet.

Of

Of Abſtinence.

CHAP. IIII.

FOR ſo much as it is contained in the forme of life, that the Siſters ought to faſt at all times; vve ſay conſequently, that they ought to abſtaine at all times and in all places from eating fleſh. And although in the forme of life be contained this clauſe; to wit, that on Chriſtmas day, on what day ſoeuer it falleth, the Siſters may mak two refectiõ ; we declare that therby it is not graunted vnto them, that on the ſaid day they may eate fleſh, no more then on al Sundaies, on which the Siſters may alſo al in

common

common make two refections, as
all Christians doe on the Sundaies
of Lent, according to the custome
and ordinance of our holy Mother
the Church.

2.   It is also contained in the
same forme of life, that with the
young, & weake the Abbesse shall
mercifully dispēce as she thinketh
good; whereupon it is to be noted, that in this dispensation one
cannot commonly well determine
the necessity of the age, or weaknes, sith it happeneth oftentimes,
that some are more strong at 15.
yeares, then others at 16. and some
also more grieued and weakned
with a short and light sicknes, then
others are vvith a grieuous and
long sicknes; for which cause we
exhort them all in our Lord, that

in

in all things they carry themfelues
fo prudentlv, that amongft them
doe more shine the charity of Iefus Chrift, then ouer great & indif-
creet aufterity : in fuch fort neuertheles , that the Abbeffe alfo doe
not to eafilv difpenfe without true
neceffity , becaufe by fuch difpen-
fatiós many times there haue come
great relaxatió, in fome Religions.

5. The Abbeffe neuerthelesfe,
or her Vicareffe, by the counfell
of the difcreet may difpenfe with
the young, ficke , and weake, that
they may take their refection oftentimes in a day, when true and
iuft neceffity requireth it , for
wnome alfo they fhall fufficiently
prouide in their necefïityes or
weaknes , as well in meate as in o-
ther thinges.

D   4. Fur-

4. Further we ordaine that the Abbeſſe haue diligēt care, that with the almes which come vnto her, ſhe prouide competently for the Siſters in common, according to to quantity of almes, to the end that the ſiſters haue not occaſion to deſiſt, and giue ouer their vertuous beginings, and holy exerciſes, for want of common, or ſufficient refections.

Of Confeſſion, and of Communion :
of the Confeſſour and his Com-
panions.

C H A P. V.

TO the end that amongſt the Siſters of this Order purity of hart & body may haue vigour,

gour, and be nourished, and that
the loue and deuotion, vnto the
most holy Body of our Lord, be
alwaies augmented and increased:
we will and ordaine, that aboue,
the number mentioned in their
forme of life (to wit that the Sisters
with leaue of the Abbesse doe confesse twelue times in the yeare) e-
uery Sister who shall not be lawfully hindred, may confesse twice
euery weeke, and likewise as often
(besides the seauen times written
in the forme of life) shall receaue
with the greatest deuotion they are
able, the pretious Body of our
Lord, in the Conuentuall Masse,
except with leaue of the Abbesse or
the counsaile of the Confessour of
the Couent, any would deferre or
abstaine from the said communion

vntill

vntill another day , for some iust
cause ; admonishing them strictly
to haue a great and particular care,
that they doe it with the best preparation , and greatest reuerence
they shall be able , to the end they
doe not vndertake so great a work
through custome, but with seriour
of spirit .

2 .   Likewise we will , and also
commaund by Obedience, that no
Sister (of what condition so euer
she be) may presume, to confesse to
any Confessour , Religious , or secular of what degree, condition,or
dignity soeuer he be , vnder coul-
iour of any grace , or priuiledge
graunted to the one , or other ,
then vnto the Confessour of the
Couent, except the Abbesse by the
counsaile of the greatest part of the

dis-

difcreet fifters, & that for iuft & re-
fonable caufe, giue leaue vnto her.

3. Againe we ordaine, that
after the laft peale is rung vnto
Compline, vntill after Tierce, no
Sifter may go to Confeffion without neceffity.

4. And notvvithftanding,
that in the forme of life it be contained, that it is lawfull for the
Chapline, to celebrate Maffe within the monaftery, to communicate the ficke Sifters; neuertheleffe
for many perils, daungers, and in-
conueniences, that heer by might
ariue vnto the Sifters; we commaund all Abbeffes and Portreffes
and all others prefent and to come
of euery place, and Couent, that
they neuer permit any Prieft, Reli-
ous, or Secular, to celebrate with
D 3   in

in their Cloiſter, or to Communicate either ſicke, or ſound, except
any of them vvere oppreſſed vvith
ſome grieuous ſicknes, or long
contagious diſeaſe, through which
ſhe could not, or it were not conuenient, for ſome great daunger, that
ſhe ſhould come to Maſſe, or receaue the body of our Lord with
the others in the Church: then in
ſuch a caſe we grant, that in the
ſeauen tymes ordayned in the
forme of life, and more often, if
the Abbeſſe with the counſaile of
the Diſcreet, do find it conuenient, and for the conſolation of the
ſicke, the Confeſſour with his Cō-
panion, may, for this adminiſtra-
tion, enter within the Cloiſter.

   5. Further, although it be contained in the ſayd forme of life,
                              that

that the Sisters shall haue mercifully a Chaplaine of the Order of the
Friar-Minors , vvith a Clarke of
good name, and discreet, and two
lay Brothers, louers of holy con-
uersation and modesty , for ayde
of their Pouerty ; we declare that
the sayd words ought to be vnderstood in the manner following : to
wit,that the Sisters in euery couent
haue , or may haue , if they haue
need , foure Brothers of the Order
of the Friar-Minors, of whome the
first and principall,shall be a Priest
their Chaplaine & Confessour,who
ought to be pious,prudent,deuout
and discreet, and well approued in
Regular obseruance, not to young
but of a conuenient age: the second
shall be his companion , who must
not only be a Clarke , but also a
D 4   Priest

Priest of good name, prudent and diſcreet, vnto whome the Confeſſour of the Siſters may confeſſe ſo often, as it is needfull: the other two ſhall be lay Brothers, & ought to be, as the forme of life ſaith, zelatours of holy conuerſation, and modeſty.

6. Which foure Brothers, the Abbeſſe of euery Couent ought by the couſaile of the Diſcreet humbly to demaund, and require, of the grace and fauour of the Reuerend Father Miniſter-Generall, or of the Prouincialls, or their Vicars, and the ſaid ſayd miniſter Generall for all the Couents of the ſayd Siſters, or the Prouinciall-Miniſters, or their Vicars for the Couents which are ſcituated in their Prouinces & Vicaries, oughe merci-

mercifully, in regard of the piety of our Lord, and of S. Francis, to condescend vnto their said Postulation and request, and to giue them the said foure Brethren, or at the least a Father with his companion, in the Couents, where the Abbesse & the Sisters haue no need of lay Brothers.

Of the obseruance of Cloister.

CHAP. VI.

POPE Innocent the forth hath declared that those who haue vowed to keep this Rule and manner of life, ought to keep, and obserue perpetuall Cloister; and that it shall be no more lawfull, and

D 5   that

that there be not giuen vnto them
licence or power in all the time of
their life to goe forth of the inclo-
fure of their Monaſtery , vnles it
were to build or to plant this Religion , or to reforme it in ſome monaſtery, or to take vpon them the
gouernement or correction therof,
or for to ſhunne ſome other great
danger; and that then it be with the
licence of the miniſter Generall, of
the order of the Friar-Minors , or
of the Prouinciall of the Prouince,
or of their Vicars wherin the ſaid
monaſtery ſhall be ſcituated.

2.   And when it doth hapen
that they do ſend any Siſters forth
of their monaſtery for the afore-
ſaid cauſes; we will , and ordaine
that they be accompanyed with
honeſt perſons , and fearing God,
                                    and

and that they goe vnto the other Couent assigned for them, with all speed possible.

3. Those who in this sort shalbe transported, must be carefull when they are amongst the secular, to shun all vaine and vndecent words or lookes, or full beholding of any one, but that they shew themselues mortifyed, speaking humbly, and conuersing modestly, with euery one, as it beseemeth the hand-maydes of Iesus Christ, and the daughters of S. Clare.

4. In like manner because in the forme of life mention is made of Sisters seruing without the monastery, who make profession as the other Sisters, as it is there written (except the vow of Cloister) and goe in and out, and serue the
other

Other Sisters, of thinges necessary
to be done without the monastery
as it is expedient ; neuertheles , for
many perils, and dangers which by
this occasion might come vnto the
said Sisters , and their Couents ,
Pope Bennet the tweluth hath or-
ordained, and instituted, that from
hence forward no Sister Professed
presume to goe forth of the Cloister, except for the causes mentioned in the forme of life : we likewise willing that the said ordinance
should be inuiolably obserued, doe
command , that all the Sisters of
what state and condition so euer
they be, who are bound to the obseruance of the first Rule of Saint
Clare , or shall heerafter be bound
thereunto , that they alwayes per-
seuer vnder perpetuall Cloister , in
                              such

such sort that heerafter none of the
haue faculty vnder the name of
seruants, or for any other cause, to
goe forth of the said Cloister, except, as is sayd, in the causes before
specifyed. Neuerthelesse it in time
to come the sisters shold haue need
of the help, and seruice of some
deuout women, which are modest
and discreet, and well aged, they
may receaue them vnto their help
and seruice, so notwithstanding as
they in no sort enter within the
monastery.

   5.   Further we ordaine, that in
euery Couent there be made in an
opē & cōmon place, one only strōg
Wheele, of a conuenient height &
largenes, and so compassed, that by
no clefts or creuisses, any one may
see into the Couent from without,
                     nor

nor from within forth of the same,
by which Wheele the Sisters may
receaue the things that shall be
brought vnto them, and giue forth
that which is to be giuen forth:
but if the said things were so great
and so long that they could not be
giuen in or out by the wheele, they
shall be giuen by the gate, into the
monastery, and forth by the same,
when it is expedient.

6.   In like manner for the
more surety & purity of the Sisters
and Couents, we ordaine, that in
no Couent made, or heerafter to
be made of this Order, there be by
any meanes permitted to be made,
other Wheele, Gate, or Speak-
house then the accustomed: wherfore it sufficeth that in euery Couent, and at all times, there be one
only

only Speak-houſe, with a Wheele, and one Grate, and one Gate , and that in a common and publike place.

7. Againe we ordaine, that by the Wheele be made the Speak-window, garniſhed vvith a ſtrong grate of iron, at which grate the Siſters ſhall ſpeake when it is needful, according to the manner ſet down in the forme of life, & in theſe preſent Ordinances, for iuſt occaſions.

8. In like ſort we ordaine, that within the incloſure of the Couent, right ouer agaynſt the Principall Gate , there be another Gate vvhich ſhall in ſuch ſort be placed, that the Siſters by no meanes be able to approach, or goe vnto the principall Gate , and that none from without, by reaſon of the ſecond

second gate, be able to see into the
Couét, through an creuisses, if there
should chance to be any in the first
gate, nor heare the Sisters frõ within Likwise we will, that the gardẽ
dore, and the dormitory be strongly locked in the night.

9.   For greater surety of the
sayd Sisters we ordayne, that no Sister of what condition so euer she
be, put letter of commendation, or
any other writing, eyther open, or
shut, either by herself, or by others,
at the Wheele, Grate, nor Gate,
neyther cause any to be there layd,
to the end of being sent or carryed
forth : and whatsoeuer letter there
put, or cast, or at any other part
whatsoeuer, none shall presume to
receaue, or cause to be receaued,
nor open, or read, vntill the letter
hath

hath wholy bin prefented vnto the
Abbeffe, which letters the Abbeffe
ought to reade before any Sifter doe
receaue them, and if the Abbeffe
finde any thing in the faid letters
vnfit, they fhall in no fort be giuen
vnto the Sifter to whome they are
fent, or by whō they   were fent
forth of the Couent, but the Sifter
fhall be grieuoufly punifhed, and
none fhall be permitted to put their
letters into the hands of thofe who
fhould carry them.

10. In like manner, that no Abbeffe doe read any letter, which is
fent vnto her from withcut, nor
doe fend any forth of the Monaftery to any perfon vntill the letter
haue byn prefented to one of the
Difcreete Sifters affigned for this
effect by the other Difcreet, which
        E   fifter

sister ought to be changed euery
yeare, and another ordained and
assigned in her place: which sister
thus assigned ought to reade all the
letters before the Abbesse do reade
thē, or send thē forth of the couent.

*Of the election of the Abbeße, Dis-
creete, and the other Officers.*

CHAP. VII.

NOTVVITHSTANDING
that the Rule say, That the
Sisters shall procure spedi-
ly the Minister Generall, or the
Prouinciall of the Friar-Minors,
who may with the word of God,
exhort them vnto concorde, and
vnion, and to seeke the common
profit,

profit, in the election of the Abbesse; we neuertheles, considering
the many affaires of the Superiors,
as also the continuall occupations
of the sayd Generall and Prouinciall, in respect of the gouernement
and care of their subiects; for these
and many other iust reasons, ordaine, that they being hindred by
any busines, may giue charge vnto
any other Father whome they shall
iudge sufficient for that affaire.

2. To the end that in this election the sisters may proceed more
securely, we will and ordaine, that
when the Abbesse of any Couent
shall be departed forth of this life,
or detayned with any long infirmity, in such sort that she could not
well exercise her office, or that she
for some iust and reasonable cause,

would renounce the said Office, or
that she were a violator of the Rule
and holy Obseruance , or found
culpable in any enormous crime ,
or hainous offence, presently three
dayes after her death,deposing, or
absolution , the professed Sisters
ought to prouide theselues of another Abbesse , by Canonicall E-
lection : in which Election none
ought to be chosen for Abbesse , if
she be not 30. yeares of age,& haue
expresly vowed the forme of life ,
and bin well tryed therin.

3. When they haue that election to make, they shall hold this
order. First the 3. day after her
death,the Vicaresse shall certify the
Superiour who then resideth in
the Prouince , by a letter or mes-
senger of the death , or deposition
of

of their Abbeſſe, beſeeching him to
come, or to ſend one to make the
Election of another Abbeſſe ; and
in the meane time whileſt they ex-
pect his comming, the Siſters ſhall
make continuall & feruent prayer
vnto Almighty God, beſeeching
him to diſpoſe all things to the honour and glory of his diuine maie-
ſty.

4. We command by hol-
ſome Obedience, that the Siſters
doe not ſpeake vnto ech other a-
bout the election, as it were to coū-
ſaile, or ſay, It ſeemeth vnto me
that ſuch a one is fit, or, What do
you thinke of ſuch a one ; but that
euery one doe leaue the affaire vn-
ſo the inſpiratiō of the holy Ghoſt,
and that they take great heede in
all their elections to proceed pure-

ly, sincerely, holily, and Canonically, without cauillation; and that being altogeather vnited in peace and charity, they choose her whom they know to be fittest for the saluatió of soules, & profit of the monastery.

5. To the end that the Sisters may be more vnited & conformed vnto the diuine will, and may the better know it, the same morning the Election is to be made, the Sisters shall communicate if it be possible, and the same morning also Masse shall be sayd of the holy Ghost. And note that the Vicaresse ought to write, or cause to be written all in one hand, two or three times, as many bills in number, as there are Sisters professed, vvherein these vvordes shall be written,

written . I choose for our Reuerend Mother Abbeſſe Sister N. and
the Vicareſſe ſhall giue vnto euery
Sister one of the ſaid bils , wherein
euery Sister ſhall write the name
of her whome ſhe iudgeth according vnto God and conſcience , to
be the fitteſt to exerciſe that office ;
When the Superiour or Viſitour ,
or he who ſhal be aſſigned to make
the ſaid Election, ſhal be entred into the Chapter-houſe, al the Sisters
being there aſſembled, he ſhal mak
them an exhortation concerning
the election : that being done , all
the Sisters ſhall depart out of the
Chapter-houſe , and returne one
by one to the Superiour , giuing
him their bill , wherin they haue
written the name of her whome
they chooſe : & hauing all deliue-
E 4   red

red their bils, they shall agayne all
togeather enter into the Chapter-
house, and the Prelate who hath
receaued the bils shall pronounce
the voyces, begining with her who
hath the fewest, vntill they be all
ended, and she who shall be found
to haue the most voyces (more
then the halfe) shalbe truly elected.
And if peraduenture she should
not be elected at the first, they shall
againe returne vnto the election, in
the same manner, vntill she be
chosen: and thus in euery Election, it is necessary, and it sufficeth,
to haue more then halfe the voices:
She being chosen, and the voices
pronounced by the Superiour, he
shall confirme her in the name of
the Father, of the Sonne, and of the
Holy Ghost. Amé. That being done
                              they

they shall say , *Te Deum Laudamus*: and at the end the Prelate sayth , *Confirma hoc Deus* , and the prayer *Actiones:* & after all the Religious shall go & imbrace their new Mother , & shall acknowledge her for their true, and lawfull Abbesse, and Superiour .

6. The same manner ought to be held in the election of the Vicaresse, and all other Officers , excepting that they shall only name the by voices without writing any thing . And to the end that peace , loue . & truth of good conscience may alwaies remaine amongst the said Sisters, we admonish the in our Lord Iesus Christ , that in all their elections , mutations , & changing of the officers and discreet , they shunne all ambitions , discordes ,

E 5   malice ,

malice, and euill affection, in pro-
moting the vnfittest, and deposing
the worthiest and most sufficient,
for therby they should hurt their
one consciences very much.

8.   Contrariwise that none of
them being chosen by the will of
the holy Ghost, & voyce of the
Sisters, vnto any Office, do refuse
the paine and labour; but that for
the loue of our Lord, they humbly
accept it, and exercise it with diligence, according to the grace which
God shall giue them; and that they
doe not demand to be absolued or
deposed from their office, without
great, and reasonable cause, and by
sound and good counsaile; and
that in exercising their office they
alwaies haue good patience, and
charitable sufferance: for he, for
whose

whose loue they doe it , will giue
and distribute vnto them , euerlasting reward .

The manner to hould Chapter.

CHAP. VIII.

FOR so much as according to
the forme of life, the Abbesse
is bound to call her Sisters vnto Chapter at least once a weeke:
to the end that this may be euery
where and alwaies obserued , we
appoint and ordaine , that the Abbesse , or Vicaresse be carefull to
assigne such an houre to hold the
said Chapter , that ait the Sisters in
health may come vnto it . Besides
which Chapter , there may be added, one or two , euery weeke according to the number of Sisters ,
and

and diuersity of affayres; and for this, there shall be nothing omitted of the diuine Office, or of the other common offices.

2. As often as the Abbesse vvould gather her Sisters vnto Chapter, the bel of Obedience shal be only tolled, and then all the Sisters in health who are not for that present necessarily occupyed, or in the seruice of the sicke, shall be bound so soone as they heere the signe of the bell, to come vnto all the assemblies.

3. The Abbesse or Vicaresse, after the inuocation of the holy Ghost, shall make the generall recommendations for the liuing and the dead, naming in particular the benefactours which haue bestowed any almes vpon them : which

recom-

recommendations being made, the Sisters rise vp, saying the suffrages for thē, to wit , *A d te leuaui occulos meos*. *De profundis clamaui*, with the suffrages which follow , *Pater noster*, ℣. *Et ne nos*. ℞. *Sed libera* ℣. *Fi..t pax &c.* and at the end they shall say *Pater noster*, & the Abbisse, *Deus det nobis suam pacem* . *A-men.*

4. Then the Abbesse and all the Sisters doe againe sit downe, and if there be Nouices they must first speake their fault, and hauing receaued pennance of the Abbesse or her Vicaresse , depart forth of the Chapter , and goe into the Church, and pray for the other.

5. They being departed, all the professed togeather shall pro-strate themselues , and speake their
faults

faults in generall , and for the fame
receaue generall pennance : and
after that , euery one in particular
fhall acknowledge their fault humbly , and deuoutly , as they find
themfelues to haue fayled , & that
with ioyned hands, and vpon their
knees , proftrate on the ground ,
beginning at the yongeft : & then
the Abbeffe , or her Vicareffe doth
impofe them pennance, euery one
according to the greatnes of the
fault committed ; and if it be
needfull fhe doth admonifh , reprehend, and correct them charitably , as fhe fhall thinke expedient,
without fhewing any partiality: &
the Sifters ought always to receaue
the fayd pennance , with all humility and patience , & accomplifh it
with deuotion .

6. And

6. And let all the Sisters, take very great heede, that they neuer make any Reply in Chapter, or els where, or any couered excuse; and that none be so bolde as to speake there, without the leaue of the Abbesse.

7. Let the Sisters take likewise heed, that they do in no sort vpraide ech other of the faults corrected in Chapter, or Visitation, nor any other defectes committed in the world, and if heerein any one should be found faulty, she shalbe seuerely punished by the Abbesse.

8. All things then being accopli-shed & finished, as hath byn sayd, if they haue any busines to treate of according to the forme of life, they may speake therof togeather, and
that

that with expedient & due grauity,
& modesty , taking carefully heed
to themselues , that they doe not
there speake, or vtter any disordinate, superfluous , or vnprofitable
wordes: and all thinges thus ac-
cōplished , the Abbesse making the
signe of the Crosse, sayth: *Adiuto-*
rium nostrum in nomine Domini. R̵.
Qui fecit &c. and so they depart
forth of Chapter, in the name of
our Lord.

Of silence, and the manner of spea-
king at the Speake-house, and
at the Grate.

CHAP. IX.

FOR as much as peace is the
worke of Iustice, and silence
the gard and keeper of the said
peace, to the end that the feruour
of deuotion, grow not cold, and be
not extinguished by disordinate &
ouer much talke, we ordaine that
the Sisters keepe silence as it is contayned in the forme of life, to wit
from after Compline, vntill Tierce
of the next morning be read.

2. They shall keep continuall
silence as the forme of life saith, in
F   the

the Church, Dormitory, and in the
Refectory when they eate, except
in the Infirmary.

3. And although in the sayd
forme of life their be no mention
made, that they shall keep silence
in the Cloifter; the reason may be
that in the time of S. Clare when
S. Francis gaue her the forme of
life in the monaftery of S. Damian,
where she remained, they had then
no Cloifter, by reason of the great
pouerty of the place: we neuertheles diligently cófidering that Pope
Gregory the ninth ordained, in the
firft Rule, that the sayd Sifters,
should keep continuall silence, at
all times, and in all places, and
likewise becaufe in all Religions
well ordered the Cloifter is the firft
place next vnto the Church, where
they

they are accustomed to keep silence; we institute, and ordaine, that from hence forward all the Sisters keepe alwayes silence, in the Cloister, as in the other place, named in the forme of life.

4. Further we command, that no Sister of what office degree or condition soeuer she be, doe goe vnto the Speake-house without licence of the Abbesse or her Vicaresse, and also that no Sister hauing leaue to govnto it in any sort, speak to any person at the sayd Speake-house, except there be present two professed Sisters plainly hearing & vnderstanding that which they say; and they must be of the number of the eight Discreet of the Couent. For seeing that at the grate in the Church where they are in the pre-

F 2   sence

sence of Almighty God, and his Angels, there must be three of the said Discreet assigned; how much greater reason is there, that the Speake-house which is a more common and publike place, there should be two of the number of the sayd Discreet assigned vnto that Sister, who ought to speake, hauing leaue of the Abbesse, for any reasonable cause.

5. Likewise we ordaine, that no Sister doe euer speake at the Gate of the Couent, with any person from without, neither aloud nor softly, nor with her companions, or without them.

6. Further we wil & ordaine, that when any Sister for any euident profit or necessity, or for any reasonable cause, ought to speake

at

at the Grate which is in the Church
vnto any perſon , before and after
ſhe beginneth to ſpeake , one ther-
unto appointed may a little hold
vp the Curtine , which hangeth
within , and preſently to let it fall
downe againe in the accuſtomed
place, in ſuch ſort that whē ſhe ſpea-
keth , ſhe be neuer ſeene by any
perſon in the face, & no Siſter ſhall
ſpeake there except as the forme
of life ſaith, vnto perſons of accoūt
which are mature and modeſt , or
their neereſt Parents & kindred or
ſpirituall friendes , and that very
ſeldome .

7. If it ſhold happē that any perſon were to enter in & ſpeake with
them , they ſhall couer modeſtly
their faces , and decline a little , as
it appertaineth vnto the modeſty

F 3   of

of Religion.

8.   Furthermore in S. Mar-
tins Lent (which we will haue to
begin the day after all-Saints day,
and to laſt vnto the Natiuity of our
Lord) & in the great Lent (which
we will haue to begin the day after
Quinquageſima, and laſt vntill Ea-
ſter) that no Siſter within theſe
tymes ſpeake at the ſpeake-houſe,
or at the grate vnto any perſon, except (for the cauſes contayned in
the forme of life) the Abbeſſe, or
her Vicareſſe, & the Portreſſe only,
for the profitable buſines of the
Couent, as vnto this preſent, it
hath bin accuſtomed.

9.   In like manner, within this
time no Siſter ſhall write vnto her
Parents, or friendes, except it
be vpon ſome extraordinary occaſion,

fion, that cannot be deferred, the which shall be committed vnto the discretion of the Abbesse.

10. Againe we exhort them in our Lord Iesus Christ that when any Sister doth speake at the grate in the Church, or at that in the Speake-house (for at the wheele it may not be permitted) that she take heed of prolixe, vayne, vnprofitable, and worldly wordes, but that the wordes which proceede from their mouth, be holy, modest, and profitable, as beseemeth the handmaides of our Lord Iesus, and the obseruers of the holy Ghospell.

11. To shun the suspitions & familiarities of secular persons, and their long and vnprofitable discourses, we ordaine that the Sisters

E 4   be

be in no fort God-mothers vnto a-
ny man or vvoman Child , by
themfelues , or by any perfon in-
terpofed .

11 .   Further we ordaine, that
when it is needfull for any to enter into the Cloifter,either to vifite
the fick,or for any other iuft caufe,
the Sifters vvhich haue leaue to
fpeake, fhall not fpeake vnto them
but in the prefence of two Sifters ,
which muft heare them, and they
muft be of the number of the difcreet,& affigned by the Abbeffe or
her Vicareffe, for this effect .

Of

Of the obſeruance of Pouerty ; and that the Siſters may not admit any poſſeſſions , nor haue any thing proper .

CHAP. X.

FOR ſo much as according to the forme of life , the Abbeſſe, and all the Siſters , are bound to obſerue Pouerty , which they haue promiſed vnto God and vnto S. Francis, to wit, not receauing or hauing poſſeſſions , or propriety , by themſelues, or by any perſon interpoſed ; to the end they may obſerue the ſavd pouerty , more perfectly and intierly in not recceauing or detayning any poſſeſſions , or

F 5   proprie-

propriety; we forbid by obedience
the said Sisters, in any sort to receaue any house to hire, or land, or
garden to plough, or medow to till
or vineyard, or any other thing, to
manure, or possesse.

2. Furthermore they shall not
haue inheritances or rents, nor shal
not receaue yearly prouisions, or
perpetuall almes eyther by themselues, or by any other person in-
terposed. Likwise not to haue gra-
naries, or cellers so full of thinges
bought or begged, or otherwise
gained, in so great plenty and a-
boundance, that they should sell
of the said prouision, or be therewith able to passe their life a whole
yeare, without begging: this doth
wholy repugne vnto their pouerty.

3. They

3. They fhall alfo neuer haue oxen, kyne, or flocks of fheep, or ftable of horfes, nor cuppes or difhes of gold, or filuer, or any other pretious thinges : likewife Ieuuelis of gold, or filuer, or money, or pretious ftones, or any other thinges, or prouifions vvhich may laft aboue a yeare : all thefe are prohibited vnto them.

4. Furthermore we wil, that in all their garments, aparell, veffells, furniture, and in all thinges as well of the Church as otherwife, they fhunne all curiofity, and fuperfluity, to the end that in them alwaies may fhine the holy pouerty, and amongft thé euer raigne the neceffity and fpare vfe of thinges, as it appertaineth vnto thofe who ought to follow the moft holy Pouerty. 5. Fur-

5: Further we will and ordaine, that with the thinges which are giuen vnto the Sisters in Wills, or Testaments they do in such sort as Pope Nicolas the third hath ordained, in the declaration of the Rule of the Friar-Minors.

6. Againe, seing that the forme of life saith, that the Sisters shall appropriat nothing to themselues, neither house, nor place, nor any other thing. And by the said Pope Nicolas the third, and Clement the fifth, and many other most holy Fathers, it hath bin declared in the declarations of the Rule of the Friar-Minors, that the renuntiation and abandoning of all thinges, which the said Brothers do make, ought to be vnderstood and obserued aswell in particular, as in common

mon ; and we in this article adhe-
ring vnto the aforesaid writing,
will and command the said abandoning, and renuntiation of the propriety of all thinges, which the Sisters do make for the loue of God
(as meritorious, and profitable, &
worthy of eternall retribution) to
be entierly & inuiolably obserued
of all the said Sisters present, and
to come, as well in particular as in
common : neuertheles the said Sisters may, with a safe conscience,
haue the bare vse of al things, which
are graûted according to the forme
of life, and of those which are not
therin forbiddê them, without the
propriety of them, as the vse of
thinges necessary for the celebration and vpholding of the diuine
office.

7. For

7. For the habitation and nou-
rishment of the body, and for the
execution of the offices, and affaires which are necessary vnto thē
according to the said forme of life,
and their holy Religion, they may
also haue the vse of such thinges as
are freely giuen or procured them
for Gods sake; and likewise of those
which they haue gained by the labour of their handes; since those
things which are giuen, begged, or
gained doe not repugne vnto pouerty.

3. Further we ordaine, that the
Almes or thinges giuen in particular, or sent vnto the Sisters shall be
distributed, in particular, or in cōmon vnto those who haue need according to the discretion of the Abbesse; and we will not haue it to be
law-

lawfull for any Sifter, to giue that which is fent vnto her, or giuen her by her parēts or friends, vnto any other needy Sifter, or to fend it to any other perfon forth of the Couent, without the liking & expreffe leaue of the Abbeffe.

9. Further we will, that concerning the debtes which are to be made, that the Sifters do alwayes, and in all times, as it is contained in the forme of life.

10. Againe, we command thē to take great heede not to make ftately & fumptuous buildings, but that they content themfelues with thofe which are meane & humble.

Of

Of the Sicke Sisters.

CHAP. XI.

VVE ordaine, that vvhen any Sister shall be grie-uously sicke, or very weake, the Abbesse or her Vica-resse shall be bound presently to prouide her of conuenient seruice: and the Sisters which are deputed to serue the sicke shall take great heede that they doe not commit a-ny notable defect in their offices, but that they serue them humbly, deuoutly & in feruour of charity, euen as they would be serued, if themselues were sicke.

2. Likewise the Abbesse if she
be

be not lawfully hindred, ſhall be
bound at the leaſt once euery day ,
to viſit the ſicke Siſters , and in her
abſence the Vicareſſe is bound to
doe it , to the end that by their negligence the ſicke Siſters doe not
want any thing in their ſicknes .

3. The Abbeſſe and her Vicareſſe , ſhall take heed that they doe
not aſke Counſell for the recouery,
and health of the ſicke Siſters of a-
ny Phiſitian, or Surgeon , which
is not a Catholike , and they ſhall
always ſend for remedy vnto the
deuouteſt , which are to be found,
but they ſhall let none of them to
enter into the Cloiſter, but for iuſt
neceſſity , and ſicknes, and thoſe
who are to enter ſhall be alwayes
duely accompanied , in ſuch ſort ,
that the Abbeſſe , or her Vicareſſe,

G Qr

or two or three Difcreet of the Couent, be alwaies prefent, vntill they
be departed forth of the Cloifter.

4. Againe, if it fhould happen
that any Sifter, or many fhould be
fick of any grieuous difeafe, as the
Leprofy, or any weaknes of head,
or lightnes of vnderftanding, or
for other fuch like ficknefles, for
which they could not conueniently remaine with the others, there
fhalbe prouided for them a chamber a part, within the Couent, and
for their conuenient feruice as their
ficknes doth require, in fuch fort
that none do euer goe forth of the
Cloifter.

5. Further, we exhort in our
Lord all the Sifters prefent and to
come, that for the loue of God, &
for the bitter death and paffion of

our

our Sauiour Iesus Christ, they will not loath or disdayne to serue those who shall be so sicke, but that humbly and deuoutly as it shall be needfull, they exhibit vnto them, all humanity, and charitable seruice.

6. If the Abbesse, or her Vicaresse, or the other Sisters deputed vnto the seruice of the sicke, do not prouide for them according to their condition, and quality, & according to the possibility of the place, in counsaile, in meate, and other thinges necessary, they shall be accused by all the other Sisters vnto the Visitour in the time of visitation, & be grieuously punished, as cruell, if they commit any notable default in the seruice of the said sicke.

7. It is alſo contained in the forme of life, to wit according to Pope Innocent the fourth, that the Siſters which are ſicke not of any long or grieuous ſickneſſe, ſhall lye vpon ſackes filled with chaffe, and ſhall haue a cuſhion of feathers vnder their heads; but if peraduenture there were ſome ſicke, of any grieuous, or long ſicknes, or for any other reaſonable, and lawfull cauſe that they could not reſt vpon the ſayd chaffe-beds, it behooueth otherwiſe to prouide for them, according vnto God and the counſaile of the Diſcreet; and therfore we will and ordayne that when it ſhall happen that any, or many ſicke of ſuch a ſicknes, the Abbeſſe, or her Vicareſſe doe prouide, or cauſe to be prouided with

the

the counfell of the Difcreete , fea-
ther-beddes , for the faid ficke, and
other thinges neceffary for them to
reft vpon , according to the forme
of life , & alfo as they in their confcience fhall thinke it to be needful,
and as the infirmity of the faid fick
doth require ; and they fhall caufe
them to reft vpon the faid beddes
with al humanity, as it fhal be expedient vnto their infirmity .

8 . The Abbeffe alfo , or her
Vicareffe , or the other Sifters deputed vnto the feruice of the ficke,
fhall diligently prouide, that when
any depart forth of this life , at the
time of her departure fhe fhalbe
cloathed with the Habit of the Order, and girded with the Cord, and
the Vaile vpon her head , and fhall
be buryed fo cloathed .

G 3   9. Againe

9.   Againe it is contained in the
forme of life, that those who haue
neede of wollen sockes, may vse
them; the which words are dispen-
satory, when necessity doth require
it: and therfore we ordaine that no
Sister of what office or condition
soeuer she be, in time of health,
weare socks, if she haue not actuall
necessity; the which necessity is not
to be determined according to the
iudgment of euery Sister, but by
the Abbesse with the counsaile of
of the Discreet, or of the greatest
part of them; which Abbesse when
she shall see some stand in neede of
sockes, or that they doe request
her to dispense with them, then if
it seeme needfull vnto the Abbesse,
and the Discreet, and that there be
manifest necessity, the conditions
                                            of

of the party prudently confidered,
& the diuerfity of times & places,
fhe fhall difpenfe with them , to
weare wollen fockes, during the
time of the faid neceffity ; and if
greater neceffity fhould arife , fhe
may alfo difpenfe with them , to
weare leather foles vvith wollen
fockes .

Of the manuall workes of the Si-
fters .

CHAP. XII.

FOR fo much as the forme of life
faith, that the Sifters vnto whō
God hath giuen the grace of
vvorking, fhall worke after the
Tierce; to the end that this may

G 4   be

be better obferued of al the Sifters,
we will , that for the loue of God
they doe not refufe the offices of
charity , and humility , but when
the Abbeffe or her Vicareffe fhall
haue inioyned them any of the faid
offices , for the common , or particular profit of the Couent , they
fhall receaue it willingly & fweet-
ly , without any murmuration or
contradiction, and with great diligence they fhal accomplifh it faithfully and deuoutly , as it hath byn
commanded them .

2 .   When in the forefayd
manner , by the Abbeffe , or her
Vicareffe, any of the forfaid things
fhall be inioyned , none of them
being found of body and vnderftanding , fhall couer themfelues
with the cloake of negligence , or
               flouth-

flouthfulnes, or pride, in saying,
God hath not giuen me the grace
to doe such and such a worke : but
they shal be humble and obedient,
as it beseemeth those who haue
vowed intiere obedience to the wil
of those who doe command them.

3. The Abbesse, and her Vicaresse ought to take great heed,
that they doe not command them
any thing, which they know pro-
bably, or manifestly, that they
could not, or are not able to doe.

4. Although in the said forme
of life it be said, that the Sisters shal
worke after the Tierce ; we neuertheles considering the straite pouerty of the said Sisters, and the necessity and want which they may
haue, graunt that if there should be
in the Couent, any necessary or

G 5   conue-

conuenient worke to be done before the said houre, that the Abbesse or her Vicaresse, may command those whome they thinke
good to doe the said workes, or to
finish them, if they be begun.

5. Againe we command the
said Sisters that none of them from
hence forward presume, to make,
or to finish any worke for their Order, or for any other person of
what condition soeuer, or in what
sort soeuer, by which iustly they
might be noted of vanity & curiosity; when it is needfull for the Sisters to doe any such worke, before
it be accepted, or begun, it shall
be wholy presented vnto the Abbesse, or her Vicaresse, who ought
to iudge whether the worke be fit
to be done by the Sisters or not, &
nothing

nothing fhall be done without her
liking, or permiffion: and the Sifters which fhall doe the contrary,
fhall be punifhed according to the
difcretion of the Abbeffe or Vicareffe.

6. Againe, after the Maffe, at
a conuenient tyme, they may ring
vnto worke, & then all the Sifters
which haue no lawfull excufe, fhal
come to do the worke which is appointed, and enioyned them.

7. Furthermore, we ordaine,
that all the Sifters prefent and to
come, do alwayes, and in all places
abftaine from all fecular, & vaine
paftimes, and from all worldly
vaine playes of what thing, or in
what fort foeuer they be.

8. When two, or many, are
togeather, if they haue leaue to
fpeake

speake, and recreate (for otherwise they must keep silence) they
shall speake alwaies of God, and
of the liues of Saints eyther liuing
or dead, or of somthing belonging
to the health of their soules, or of
some decent and profitable busines, and that they take great heed
of all idle, hurtfull, and dissolute
wordes, as it becometh the handmaides of Iesus Christ, and obseruers of the holy Ghospell, and the
professours of holy Religion.

9. Further, vve forbid the
Sisters to haue or keep in their Couent, or to reade, or write, or
cause to be written, any Bookes
wherein there should be expresly
contained any open, or secret vanity, or carnality, or history of
worldly persons : neuertheles it is
law-

lawfull for them , to haue holy
bookes in their Couents in common for the comfort and profit of
their foules , which they may read
in particular , or in common , at
the table , or in any other place, according to the will & appointment
of the Abbeſſe.

Of the correction of the faulty.

CHAP. XIII.

VV E ordain, that in euery
Couent , the Abbeſſe ,
or in her abſence the
Vicareſſe, doe admoniſh and correct the Siſters humbly , and charitably , to the end that they doe
not fall into the pitt of tranſgreſſi-
on ,

on, for want of correction and admonition; so that the said Superiours keep (as is ordained in the said correction) true charity, and sweet humility.

2. They shall also take heed that vnder the colour of humility and sweetnes, they doe not giue the Sisters occasion of liberty and relaxation; and vnder the shadow of charity, nourish true carnasity of the body, and cruelty to the soules; but they shall correct them all equally as it is expedient, without any difference, according to their faults.

3. If it should happen (which God forbid) any Sister had committed so great a crime, or enormous sinne, that she had put her soule in daunger of perdition, and her

her Order in infamy, & confusion,
or if there were any so rebellious,
incorrigible, or perseuerant in her
malice, so that she would in no
sort amend; for such there shall be
made in euery Couent, a chamber
of discipline, strong but humane,
wherin she shall be put & kept for
a certaine time with bread and water, as fifteene dayes, a moneth, a
yeare, or perpetually, according
as the offence doth require it, and
according to the discretion of the
Abbesse & the Discreet.

4. Againe if it should happen
that any Sister should rebell a-
gainst the Abbesse or Vicaresse, &
should say vnto them any vndecent and iniurious words, she shall
eate bread and water only, sitting
on the ground before all the Sisters

sters, the space of a whole refection.

Of the Portreſſe, and entring into the Monaſtery.

CHAP. XIIII.

ALTHOVGH in the forme of life it be contained, that the Portreſſe shall keep her reſidence the day tyme, in an open Cell without a dore: we neuertheles for many iuſt occaſions moouing vs heere vnto, will not haue that this be now obligatory, nor that it be by any meanes obſerued; for although in the time of Saint Clare, it was decent and lawfull for the Siſters, neuertheles it might be now very hurtfull & perilous vnto them.   2. Ther-

2. Therefore we deſiring to prouide for their ſecurity and de-cency, Ordaine that they obſerue the manner following, to wit, that there be deputed a Siſter, fearing God, to keepe the Gate of the Mo-naſtery, and the Speak-houſe, one who is moderate, of good man-ners, diligent, diſcreet, and of con-uenient age, to the end that (as the forme of life ſaith) ſhe may with word and deed edify thoſe vnto whome ſhe doth ſpeake, or with whome ſhe doth conuerſeth.

3. There ſhall be aſſigned her, a fit companion by the Abbeſſe, with the counſell of the Diſcreet, who being as fit, or fitter then her-ſelfe, ſhall in the time of ſicknes, which the ſaid Portreſſe might in-cur, in all thinges fulfill her office:

H   vnto

vnto which two Portreſſes there
ſhall be aſſigned another Siſter of
the number of the eight Diſcreet
(vvhich may be changed euery
weeke, and another aſſigned in her
place) to heare thoſe who ſpeak vnto the Siſters. For no Siſter (as hath
byn ſayd) ought to ſpeake vnto a-
ny perſon from without, except
there be preſent two Siſters, of the
number of the eight Diſcreet, who
muſt heare them : which three Siſters when it ringeth ſhall come to
the chamber wherein the Wheele
and the Speak-window is placed,
in ſuch ſort, that the one doe not
ſpeake without the other two, nor
they without the third, but ſhal be
all three togeather.

4.   The principall Portreſſe
only ſhall anſwere thoſe who doe
ſpeake

speak at the Grate, & the other two
shall be present & heare her: and if
it should hapen that any one wold
speak vnto one of the other Sisters,
she or one of her companions shall
goe aske leaue of the Abbesse or her
Vicaresse to speake, and hauing licence, she who is called for, may
speake, so as there be present two
Sisters of the number of the Discreet, the principall Portresse being alwayes one, if the necessity of
some other affayre doe not hinder
her.

5. Further we ordaine, that the
said Cell or Chamber be furnished
with a dore of wood, which shall
alwayes aswell by day as by night
be locked with two keyes, vvhen
the Portresses are not within it: of
which two keyes the Abbesse shall

keep

keep one in the night,and the Portresse the other,and the third Sister
which is assigned vnto the other
two by weekes, shall keep by day
the key which the Abbesse doth
keep in the night : Within which
Speak-house none of the portresses
may enter without the other.

6. As for the entring of any
into the Monastery, we command
firmely , and strongly that no Abbesse, nor her Sisters,doe euer permit any person,Religious or secular , of what state or dignity soeuer
he be, to enter into the monastery:
and it is not lawfull for any person
whatsoeuer, except leaue were giuen them of the Popes Holines , or
of the Lord Cardinall Protector of
the Order.

7. From this law of not entring,

lring, are exempted Phiſitians and
Surgeons for iuſt neceſſity, or ſicknes; thoſe alſo who for fire, or any
other ruine, or perill, or danger, or to doe any worke which
could not be done vvithout the
monaſtery. If any Cardinall wold
enter into the monaſtery, he ſhalbe
receaued with reuerence and deuotion, but they ſhall intreate him
to enter with two or three only, of
the modeſteſt of his company.

8. Neuertheles no Siſter ſicke
nor in health, ſhall ſpeake vnto any
of thē, but in the māner contained
in the forme of life, and principally
they ſhall take heede that thoſe
which haue leaue to enter, be ſuch
that thoſe which ſee them enter,
may be edified of their liues, manners, and wordes, and that there

H 3   be

be not giuen vnto any perſon iuſt
occaſion of ſcandall.

9.   Againe we ordaine that wha
any thing is brought vnto the Couent which could not conueniently enter in at the wheele, as a barrel
of beere, or any ſuch like thing: the
Abbeſſe, or Portreſſe and her companions, ſhall take heede that the
Gate do not ſtand any longer open
then it is needfull, and they ſhall
not permit the carriers or bearers
of the ſaid thinges, to enter into
any other place of the couent, then
only into the place ſituated bet-
wixt the two Gates of the Couent
or to other places, to which of neceſſity they muſt come to place the
ſaid thinges.

10.   The Siſters ſhall take heed
that none enter beſides thoſe who
are

are neceſſary, nor permit thoſe that are entred to ſtay any longer then the worke requireth.

11. The other Siſters muſt take heed that they be not ſeene by them that enter, except thoſe who are deputed by the Abbeſſe or her Vicareſſe, and that thoſe ſpeake not with thē, but only as much as the neceſſity of the thinges requieth.

12. To the end, that this care of the Siſters not being ſeene, be the better practized, vvhen as thoſe who are to enter need not come further eyther for the worke or the bringing of any thing, then the place bētweene two Gates; we will haue them to obſerue this mā-ner, to wit, that the Portreſſes open the firſt Gate within the Couent &

H 4   enter

enter into that place to open the sea
cōd, which is the principall gate of
the Couent, the which they shall
not set wide open as the other, but
only vnlocke it with the two keyes
and lift vp the iron barre which
goeth ouerthwart, and presently
withdrew themselues vvithin the
second Gate, locking it with the
two keyes: & then those which
doe bring the said thinges may lift
vp the latch, and enter into that
place, and put the thinges there
which they do bring, and presently goe forth latching the dore after
them, & then the Portresses againe
enter in and locke the said principall Gate with the two keyes; and
and then order the thinges which
are brought in as it is conuenient.

   13. Furthermore it is contayned

ned in the forme of life, that the
Gate shall neuer be left in the day
without one to keep it. Vpõ which
we say, that for all surety it sufficeth, that the two Gates be strongly
locked as is aforesaid. And after
that, these following wordes are
written, *VVhen it is necessary that
any doe enter into the Monastery to
doe any worke, that then the Abbesse
shall appoint one to open the Gate only to those who are deputed to doe the
sayd worke, and not vnto others.* V-
pon which wordes we say, that
the said Portresse, who according
to the forme of life, ought to be
modest and discreete with those
which are assigned her for her cõ-
panions, ought to suffice to opë the
Gate vnto those who are to enter
in, to doe any worke, or for any
H 5 other

ther reasonable and iust occasions
so neuertheles that she open it with
the leaue of the Abbesse , and the
said Portresse shall then take heed
of long talke or wordes with them,
except only so much as is needfull
& conuenient for to do the worke,
for which they entred : but if it be
necessary , they may leade them
modestly and discreetly vnto the
sayd vvorke, as it shall be needfull .

14 . No Sister of what condition soeuer she be , shal euer goe to
see the workmen , or their worke
except those who are appointed by
the Abbess , for the profit of the
thing which is to be done ; and
vvhen it is needfull in this sort
to goe vnto them , they shall neuer goe without sure company of
the

the difcreet: and they shall alwaies
be in an open and common place,
and they shall not remaine longer
with them, or vfe more wordes thã
are neceffary to doe, or finifh the
faid worke.

15. The Abbeffe, and all the
Sifters shall take great heed that
they doe not caufe thofe workes
which they themfelues could doe,
to be done by ftrangers; and that
they do not permit any workmen
or others, who doe enter, of what
condition foeuer they be, to eate
within the Cloifter.

16. Further we exhort all the
Sifters in Chrift Iefus our Lord,
that they neuer be folicitous or im-
portune to procure the beneoicti-
ons of Abbeffes and confecrations
of Nunnes, but let them content
them-

themselues with their holy Profeßion, for which (if they doe well obserue it) they shall receaue the Benediction of the soueraigne Bishop our Lord Iesus Christ.

17. Againe we ordaine, that when the Confessour and his companion enter into the Monastery, that they be cloathed with sacred vestements, to wit, with the Albe or Surplisse.

18. Further we ordaine for the diuersity and difference of this present time, from that wherin the forme of life was giuen, that from hence forward there be no Masse celebrated within the Monastery neyther for the liuing, or exequies of the dead. To make the graue it shall not be lawfull for any to enter, except one or two diggers, or
masons

masons which are modest and honest : and that only in the Couents
where the Sisters cannot digge , &
close the graue as it is requisite.

19. Againe to bury the Sisters,
they shall let none enter into the
Cloister, but the Confessour & his
companion , or in the absence of
his companion , another modest
Brother : and the sayd buriall
being ended , and accomplished,
they shall presently depart forth of
the Monastery .

Of the Visitatour.

C H A P. XV.

BE I N G so that the Rule of life
setteth downe two things cō-
cerning the Visitature: the first
that

that he ought alwaies to be of the
Order of the Friar Minors; the fecond that this ought to be done by
the will and commandment of the
Lord Cardinal protector: the firſt
is yet to be obſerued, but not the
ſecond, becauſe when the Rule was
firſt inſtituted, neyther the mona-
ſteries of Siſters, nor the Siſters
theſelues were then wholy ſubiect
vnto the obedience and gouernement of the Friar-Minors; yet
notwithſtanding afterwardes, for
certaine and reaſonabble cauſes the
care and gouernement of them
hath bin wholy, and in euery reſpect committed vnto the Generall
and Prouinciall-Miniſters of the
Friar-Minors by Pope Innocent
the fourth, and diuers other holy
Bishops.

                              ΙΟ. To

2. To the end that we may more conformably proceed in the same Order by making of our Visitations; we doe ordaine, that according to the aforesaid forme of life, the said Sisters haue alwaies their Visitour of the aboue named Order of Friar-Minors, who according to the statutes of the late rehearsed Pope Innocēt the fourth, ought to be assigned and commanded by the licence and apointment of the Generall-Minister of the same order, or of the Prouinciall-Ministers within the limmits of their administrations which Visitour the Sisters ought humbly to aske, or cause to be asked for, of one of the aforesaid persons, that is to say, eyther of the Generall ouer all the Couents of the said Order, or of

the

the Prouincialls of the Couents of their Prouinces.

3. Moreouer, we doe prohibite and forbid, that the sayd Sisters doe demaund or receaue, any other for Visitour, then such a one who is well knowne and approued other Religious life, good manners and faith, as also that hath the zeale of God, and that he be an obseruer of his Rule, and louer of holy Pouerty, and of all modesty.

4. The said Visitatour is bound to visite all the Couentes which shall be committed to his charge, once a yeare, or more often, if it shall be thought necessary: as also when he shall for some reasonable and iust causes be required thereunto by the Abbesse, and other of the discreet Sisters.

5. Also

5. Also we doe Ordaine, that they neuer procure the Visitour to enter the more inward parts of the Couent, without great necessity, and this, at the time when he holdeth his Visit iuridicall & ordinary.

6. When he entreth within, to visit the Monastery he must shew himselfe such a one in all his actions, that thereby others may be mooued from good to better, and more inflamed in the loue of God, and haue alwayes mutuall Charity amongst themselues. He ought also to haue his companion with him in an open conuenient place, & so neere vnto him that the one may well perceaue and see the other without any difficulty : and that he so dispatch, that he stay no longer

I   ge

ger within the Cloifter, then during the ending of his faid bufines of Vifitation, which ended he fhall goe prefently forth of the monaftery.

7. When he fhall come to vifit any Couent, he fhall procure ahat he end his Vifite in the fpace of two or three naturall dayes: & before he beginneth the faid Vifit, it is requifite that he make an Exhortation to the Sifters, if at leaft he be prepared for it, concerning the vifit which he is to make: after this, that he reade their Rule, with this prefent Ordinance where it fpeaketh of the manner of Vifitation: next after he is to command euery one and al the Sifters, in vertue of profitable Obedience, that they anfwere him in plaine, and

good

good footh, whether they do know
any thing in thofe thinges wherof,
and wherupon he is to make in-
quifition, wherunto euery one and
all the Sifters are bound firmely to
obay in all thinges belonging to
the office of Vifitation .

8. The Vifitour may (if he fo
pleafe , and thinke it conuenient)
obferue this manner of fpeaking,
to wit , that he fpeake to all , or to
fome togeather,or with one fecret-
ly , two other Sifters being in the
place not far off in his prefence,but
not fo neere as they may heare
what is fpoken ; to the end that by
all meanes integrity may be kept:
and then the Sifters may come one
by one to giue informarions , if
there be any thing to be informed.

9. If any be accufed of any fault

or

of crime, then as well the names
of the accufers, as of the accufed
fhall be written, togeather with the
faultes they be accufed off: and the
vifit being ended, the Sifters fhall
all be called into the Chapter, afid
the faults of the accufed Sifters fhal
be declared, and a proportionable
pennance giuen vnto them, if the
crimes can be lawfully, really, and
iuridically proued by two of good
name. Neuertheles audience fhall
not be denied vnto any, to the end
that they may excufe themfelues
if they haue any lawful excufation
eyther in part or in whole; but the
accufed Sifters fhall not enquire after the names of thofe who did
accufe them, neyther fhall they by
any meanes be reuealed vnto them
except in cafe, that the accufed,

                              would

Would feeke to cleere herfelfe of
the crime wherof fhe is accufed , &
fo fhould iuridically aske that the
names of her accufers might be reuealed and knowne.

10. If it fhould happen that
any one had falfely or vniuftly accufed another, and that this might
be legitimately knowne, fhe fhall
fuftaine all that which the accufed
Sifter fhould haue fuftained, if fhe
had bin found faulty of that crime,
wherof by the other fhe was accufed. Neuertheles if fome one Sifter
in any Couent did certainly know
fome Sifters who had grieuoufly
tranfgreffed, or were at that time
in fome groffe crime, which could
not be well proued at that time; the
faid Sifter who knoweth it, may &
ought to informe the Vifitour of

I3   the

the Sifter, and of the crime, in such manner as she knoweth it, to wit secretly; and in this case the Visitour may by no meanes, at any time reueale the name of the Sifter who is the accuser, vnto her accused Sifter.

11. If any thing should at any time happen, which he of himself could not conueniently amend, he shall make relation of it vnto his soueraine Superiour, that by his Counsell and commaundment the sayd offence may be punished, according as it deserueth.

12. The Abbesse ought to be carefull, that the estate of the Monastery be not concealed, eyther by herselfe or by her Sifters from the knowledge of the Visitatour, in the obseruance of their Religion,

on, in vnity of mutuall Charity,
which they al ought to haue togeather; for this should be no small
sinne, but an offence worthy to be
grieuously punished.

13. Wherefore, we will and
cōmaund, that those thinges which
are to be corrected, and amended
according to the forme of life, eyther publikely, or secretly, they
shall propose and declare vnto the
Visitour in the best manner that
they shall be able : & if any should
doe otherwise, be she Abbesse or
whosoeuer of the rest, she is to be
punished seuerely by the Visitour,
according as she hath deserued.

14. When the Visitatour
shall make his Visit publickly or
secretly ; amongst other thinges
which he should enquire of the Si-

I 4 sters,

ſters, he ſhall firſt demaund of
thinges moſt Eſſentiall, concerning
their Rule &c. firſt of Obedience,
Pouerty, Chaſtity, and of the e-
ternall and ſtraite Incloſure. Se-
condly how they keep the diuine
Office, as well by night as by day:
then the manner of ſpeaking aſwel
at the Grate as at the Speak-houſe.
Thirdly of the gathering togeather
of money, corne, oyle, and vvine.
Fourthly of the ſeruice done to the
ſicke, weake, and very aged. Fifth-
ly of the number, richenes, and
curioſity in habits and cloathings.
Sixthly the obſeruances of abſtinence and faſtes: & of negligences
of thoſe which rule. Seauenthly,
of the Diſcreet Siſters, and of the
Portreſſes. Eightly, of the Obedience and rebellion of the ſubiects.
                              Ninthly

Ninthly, of the obseruance of their
Rule, and life, and of these present
Ordinances . Tentnly, of the peace
and vnity to be kept by the chaine
of perpetuall Charity . Eleuenthly
of the frequentation of the Sacra‑
ment of Pennance , and of the ho‑
ly Sacrament of the Aultar . Twel‑
uthly , to enquire how the sacrifice
of holy prayer and deuotion is cō‑
tinued , and preserued in the Cō‑
uent .

15 . If any one or more should
legitimately be found failing in a‑
ny of these aforesaid thinges, or a‑
ny thing which might be otherwise
notoriously defectiue , that then
she be duely corrected and puni‑
shed according to discretion , zeale
of charity , and loue of Iustice ;
and also according as the offence

I 5   hath

hath bin committed more often.

¶ BY THE HELP OF
these Declarations, Constitutions,
and ordinances, we trust by the
grace of God, to haue sufficiently
prouided for your estate; the which
by these present writings we doe
send vnto you all, and vnto euery
one of you, that you feruently &
efficaciously fulfill, and accomplish
them. And you ought by so much
the more diligently to keepe and
obserue them, by how much, we
do assuredly iudge that by the true
& entiere obseruation thereof, you
shall gaine & enioy the fruit which
is great, pretious, incomparable,
and glorious.

And to the end, that the said
Ordinances may be of greater au-
thori-

thority·, and receaued of you with greater deuotion and humility, we haue caused them to be signed, strengthened, and fortifyed, with the accustomed solemnities, as with reuiewing, examination, approbation, and the annexion of the Seale of our Office.

Giuen at *Geneua* in the Prouince of *Burgundy*, the yeare of our Lords Incarnation 1434. the eight and twentith day of September, and the third yeare of the Popedome of our holy Father Pope *Eugenius* the fourth, as also the third yeare of the holy Councell of *Basil*, gathered and assembled for the reformation of the Estates, and to procure peace betweene Princes, and for the extirpation of Heresies in which Councell these present

Ordi-

Ordinaunces, and Declarations
were viewed, examined, and approued.

*Agayne renewed, and
authorized by the Reue-
rend Father, F.*Bingnus
à Genua, *Generall of the
whole Order of our Holy
Father* S. Francis, *this
present yeare of our Lord
1622. the 22. of* Ianuary.

An

An Exhortation for the better Ob-
feruance of thefe prefent Confti-
tutions , auioyned & approued by
the Reuerend Father, F. Benig-
nus à Genua Minifter-General
of the holy Order of the Seraphi-
call Father S. Francis.

DEERLY beloued in our
Lord Iefus . It is not our in-
tentió to oblige you to your
forfaid conftitutiós vnder paine of
any fin, but only fo much as God,
your Rule, and the Church doth o-
blige

blige and bind you : Neuertheleſſe
we wil and ordaine, that the tranſgreſſours of them be ſharply corrected ; and if the Abbeſſes ſhould
be negligent to obſerue them , or
to cauſe them to be obſerued, or to
correct the tranſgreſſours, ſhe ſhall
be ſeuerely reprehended , & inioyned Pennance according to the
greatnes of her fault by the Prouincialls or Viſitours . For your holy
Mother S. *Clare* being at the article
of death , hath left the large benediction of the holy Trinity, togeather with her owne Motherly
Benediction vnto the true zealators
and obſeruers of her Rule , and of
the holy Pouerty. Wherefore you
ought to endeauour diligently to
imbrace and obſerue with affecti-
onate & ſincere loue the perfection
which

which is expreſſed and taught you
in the ſaid Rule, and in theſe holy
Ordinances, laying aſide all negligence and tepidity. And becauſe to
ſerue God with no higher intention then to auoide paine, appertaineth only vnto baſe ſeruile
ſpirits and hirelings, and to doe
things pleaſing to his diuine Maie-
ſty purely for his honour and glory, and to giue good example vnto others, for ſuch like reſpectes,
belongeth to the true Children of
God ; we exhort you all in our
Lord Ieſus to take heed that you
doe not make little account of the
tranſgreſſing of theſe preſent Conſtitutions, in reſpect that they are
not obligatory vnder paine of ſin
as we haue before ſaid;but conſide-
ſidering of what ſpirit & perfection

on they are, endeauour to obserue
them inuiolably, as the Lawes, Orders & Statutes of your Religion.
Whereby you shall add more glory to your Crowne, by meanes of
such holy indeauours, and make
your selues confomable to the Son
of God, who not being obliged or
bound to the Lawes which he had
made, would neuerthelesse obserue
them for the good of others. Seeke
then to attaine vnto the soueraigne
estate of your Religion, by infor-
cing your selues to put in execution those things which are contayned in these present Constitutions;
seing it appertayneth vnto good &
loyall Seruants not to content theselues with the fulfilling of those
thinges only, which their Maisters
comand them with treatnings, but
also.

also to seeke and desire to doe, and accomplish all such thinges which they thinke any waies to be pleasing and gratefull to their Maysters.

We doe therfore in the Charity of our Lord Iesus, exhort all the Sisters of this holy Order present and to come, that in all affaires & occasions they will keep before their eyes the holy Ghospell, the Rule which they haue promised to God, the holy and laudable customes, the memorable examples of Saints of their Order, in particular of their founders, drecting all their thoughts, words, and works, to the honor & glory of God and the health of their soules, & so doing, the holy Ghost will instruct them in all things.

K   Rayse

Rayſe, therfore your eyes and
thoughts vnto our Sweet Redee-
mer Ieſus , and hauing vnderſtood his holy wil and pleaſure, in-
force your ſelues to pleaſe him not
only in not contemning theſe preſent Conſtitutions (for the côtempt
of them were no ſmall ſin) but alſo auoiding and caſting aſide for
his loue all negligence in their obſeruance . For they will help you
not only to accompliſh intierly
your holy Rule which you haue
vowed, but alſo the diuine Law &
Euangelicall coûſailes, and obtaine
you the grace of God by Ieſuschriſt
which will deliuer you from many perills . In labours your conſolation will abound, and you ſhalbe
able to doe all thinges in him , to
wit , in Ieſus Chriſt , who is Almighty

mighty , and will comfort you , and
giue you vnderstāding in al things,
who is the wisdom of God , and giueth abondantly to euery one , and
also vvill affoard you force and
strength , seeing that it is he only
who is the strength , and the vvord
that beareth all .

Call often to mind (my deere
Sisters in our Lord Iesus) that holy
memorable Theme on which our
Seraphicall Father , made a most
worthy Sermon vnto a great multitude of Brothers , to wit , *Great
things we haue promised to God , but
greater God hath promised to vs : Let
vs thē keep what we haue promised, &
with inflamed desires, let vs aspyre to
come vnto those goods which are promised vs : the pleasures of this world
are short , but those infernall paynes*

K 2   *which*

which we get by following them, perpetuall. The sufferances we indure for the loue of Iesus Christ, and the Penance we imbrace for him, will last a little while; but the glory which God will giue vs for them, shalbe without end: many are called to the Kingdome of God, but few are choosen, because few doe follow Iesus Christ in sincerity of hart: but in the end God wil giue to euery one the recōpence of his workes, as well to the good, as to the euill, eyther glory & happynes, or confusion and eternall fire. Hitherto are the wordes of Saint Francis, the which deere Sisters may very fitly be applyed vnto you, for those thinges which you haue promised: & although they be great, yet are they small in comparison of the eternall recompence which God will giue

you

you if you be faithfull obſeruers of
them . Goe forward then , and obſerue them couragiouſly , and doè
not diſtruſt of your forces , ſeing
the eternall Father, who hath created you, & called you to obſerue the
Euangelicall perfection , knowing
well your naturall frailty, will not
only make you ſtrong and able ,
with his help, but alſo giue you his
Fatherly gifts, in ſo great multitude
add abundance , that ſurmounting
ouer all difficulties you ſhal be able
not only to obey his deerly beloued Sonne , but alſo to follow and
imitate him with exceeding great
ioy & ſimplicity of hart ; contemning perfectly theſe viſible temporall thinges , and alwaies aſpiring
vnto thoſe which are heauenly , &
eternall in Ieſus Chriſt , God and

K 3   man

man , the true light and splendour
of the glory of the eternal light, the
mirrour without spot , the Image
of God constituted by the eternall
Father, Iudge, Law-giuer and Sauiour of men, vnto whome the Father and the holy Ghost doe giue
witnes .

    Wherefore , as in him are
all our merits , our examples of
life , our aide , fauours , and re-
wardes; so likevvise let all our
thoughts , meditations, and imita-
tions, be in him; & vnto them that
so doe , all thinges will be sweet ,
pleasant, easy, light, holy & perfect.
For he is the light and expectation
of nations, the end of the Law, the
saluation of God the Father of the
world to come , and finally our
hope made vnto vs , Wisdome ,
                Iustice ,

Iuſtice , Sanctification , and Re-
demption: who liueth & raigneth
with the Father & the Holy Ghoſt
one coeternall,conſubſtantiall,and
coequall God, to whom be euerlaſting praiſe, honour, & glory . Giuen at Paris in our Couent of the
Aue Maria, this 22 . of Ianuary
1622 .

Fr. Benignus à Genua
Vicar-Generall.

K4   THE

THE

OBLIGATION

OF THE RVLE

Of our holy Mother S. Clare vnder payne of Mortall Sinne.

POPE Eugenius the 4. declareth that in the said Rule there is no other precept obliging vnder Mortall sin, then the vowes of Obedience, Pouerty, Chastity, Inclosure Election & Deposition of the Abbesse.

The

The Perfections of the Rule consist in six Seraphicall Winges, to wit, in totall Obedience, *in Euangelicall* Pouerty, *in immaculate* Chastiry, *in profound* Humility, *in Pacificall* Simplicity, *in Seraphicall* Charity.

OBEDIENCE is a Vertue which hath three degrees: the first is Obedience by profession, which is when one doth accomplish the commaundment of God, or the Prelate, touching the exteriour. The second is Obedēce by Conformity, which is when the commandment is performed not alone in the exterior, but also without murmuration, according to the

K 5   inten-

intention and wil of him that commandeth. The third is Obedience by vnion, by which he that is truly Obedient, hath no other respect but the pleasure and will of God.

2. Euangelicall Pouerty is a vertue that hath three degrees: the first is Pouerty by Profession, that is, to haue no right nor propriety in any thing whatsoeuer: the second, to retaine only the simple vse of things necessary, & rest cotented with the most vild : the third, not to haue any affection, euen in thinges necessary, but by way of constraint to take the bare vse of them.

3. Chastity is a vertue that hath three degrees : the first, Chastity of body, by which all the exterior members are restrained from any impure or suspicious act : the second
cond

cond, chaſtity of hart, by which the hart is preſerued from any diſhoneſt or vncleane thought: the third, Chaſtity of the ſpirit by which we not only refraine from any diſhoneſt loue, but alſo from al exceſſiue deiectation or ſpirituall conſolation .

4. Humility is a vertue that hath three degrees: the firſt is, Humility of knowledge, by the which man doth acknowledge to be vile and abiect in himſelfe: the ſecond is Humility of exhibitiõ, by which the interiour humility is expreſſed in the exteriour, as bv the attire , by vvordes, and by vvill , and abiect workes: the third is Humility of affection, through vvhich a ſoule doth not only humble herſelfe in the ſight of God , but alſo in the

ſight

sight of men, desiring to be esteemed poore & abiect.

5   Simplicity is a vertue which hath three degrees: the first is simplicity of thoughts, that is, not to enter into higher cogitation then the vnderstāding is capable of, neyther of honours and wordly dignities, but to esteeme himselfe the most vnworthy to serue God of all others: the second, is Simplicity in words, auoiding all affected curiosity in speach, speking plainly without superfluity; Which stil comes of an ill roote, to wit vanity: the third is Simplicity of vvorks, imploying our selues in no other but such as are simple and profitable. And a generall rule of this Vertue is to haue a pure, right, and simple intention: but Simplicity vvithout

Pru-

Prudence is not of value : for God
loueth thofe that walke in Prudence .

6.   Charity is a vertue of three
degrees: the firft is to loue God not
only for his benefits , but alfo for
that he is moft worthy of it : the fecond, is to loue our neighbour,not
only for the loue of our neighbour
but fimply for the loue of God:the
third, to loue our felues in labou-
ring for vertue , our happines, and
glory;not for our owne refpect but
for the loue of God,and to be plea-
fing vnto him .

Prayfe of the Rule .

T H E holy Father S. Francis,
encouraging his Religious to
the obferuance of the Rule,
said

said, It was the booke of life: the fruit of wifdom: the marrow of the Ghofpell: the hope of bealth: the path of faluation, the ladder by which one afcendeth to heauen: the key of Paradife: and the pledge of Eternall Peace.

Three Priuiledges, which our holy Father S. Francis obtayned of Almighty God.

POPE Gregory the Ninth faid to haue vnderftood of the holy Father S. Francis, that Almighty God had graunted him three Priuiledges: the firft that the more the Religious of his order did increafe, the more he would prouide for them: the fecond that none fhould euer vnhappily dye in the

habit,

habit: the third that whofoeuer
fhould perfecute his Order fhould
be grieuoufly punifhed by Almighty God.

*Three other Priuiledges which he
fayd to haue receaued by the Se-
raphim, when as he appeared vnto him, in the mountayne of Au-
uerne .*

THe firft, that his order fhould
laft to the day of Iudgment:
the fecond that whofoeuer
would liue wickedly in the Order
fhould not indure long : the third
that whofoeuer did loue his Order
although a great finner , he fhould
receaue and obtaine mercy of Almighty God.

Seauen

Seaue other Priuiledges which by an
Angel were reuealed vnto the ho-
ly F. S. Francis in the Couent of
S. Vrbane , to all that obserued
his Rule and dyed in the Order.

THE first, that if their intention be good, they shal euer be
gouerned by the holy Ghost:
the second, that in this their peri-
grination they shall still be par-
ticularly defended , & in all their
temptations also , from mortall sinne : the third , that the fire
of Purgatory shall not detaine
them after their death from the
immediate inioying of euerlasting
glory: the fourth, that they shall receaue in themselues that promise
of

of our Sauiour made vnto his A-
postles, of sitting on the twelue
seates to iudge the tribes of Israell:
the fifth that such as loue the Order Almighty God will increase his
graces, and blessinges towardes
them in this world and the next:
the sixth, that those who are enemies to his order, & do persecute
it without repenting, either their
life shal be shortned, or if it be long
it shalbe replenished with misery,
and after their death be eternally
lost: the seauenth that there shall e-
uer be Religious of good and holy
life, louers of the honor of God, &
their Religion in this Order.

L   Certayne

*Certayne Indulgences graunted a-
mongſt many others, by the ſoue-
raygne Bishops of Rome, vnto all
the Religious of the Order of
S. Francis.*

THE Religious both men and
women ſhall gaine a plenary
both *à pæna & culpa*, frō paine
& fault, on the daies of their Cloathing, Profeſſion, and article of
death: alſo at the article of death the
Fathers & Mothers of the ſaid Brothers & Siſters may haue the ſame
giuen thē, by any lawful Cōfeſſor.

2. All the Religious that ſhall
receaue the moſt holy Sacrament
vpon all Sundayes throughout the
yeare, all the feaſtes of our Bleſſed
Sauiour, & of our Bleſſed Lady, of
the

the Saints of the order, shall gaine a
plenary Indulgence. And if it happen that any could not confesse &
communicate these dayes, their
hindrance being lawfull, they may
gaine the same indulgence if after
being freed of that impediment,
they confesse and communicate
for that intention, notwithstāding
the day of the feast be past.

3. The Religious who shall
recite the Corone of our Lord,
that is 33. *Pater Nosters*, and *Aue
Maria*, in honour of the 33. years he
liued in the world, or the Corone
or Rosary of the Glorious Virgin
Mary, contayning 72. *Aues*, with
7. *Pater Nosters*, and one *Pater Noster* and *Aue* for the Soueraigne Bishop, do gaine plenary Indulgence.
Likewise the same is graunted as

L 2   often

often as they say the seauen Psalms and Letanies, the Gradual Psalms, the office of the dead, or assist at the Letanies of euery second Sunday in the moneth.

4. As often as the Religious eyther by day or night, in what place soeuer they be, shall recite six *Pater Nosters* and *Aues*, and *Gloria Patri*, fiue for the necessities of the Church, and the sixt for the Popes Holines, shall gaine the indulgéces of the Stations of Hierusalem, of Rome, of S. Iames, and of Portiuncula.

5. Item reciting the Psalme *Exaudiat te Dominus in die tribulationis & c.* three *Pater Nosters* and *Aues*, for the Popes intention, they shall gaine all the Indulgences graunted by the Soueraigne Bishops,

to

to the Côfraternity of the Rofary, to the Churches of our Bleſſed Lady of Loreto, of Mont-ſerat, and of Saint Iames de Compoſtella.

6. Euery time they ſay the *Angelus Domini* at the accuſtomed time when it ringeth, a plenary indulgence: and the like euery time they communicate. As often as they heare the Maſſe of the Côception of our Bleſſed Lady, praying for his Holines and the vniuerſall Church, is graunted a Plenary indulgence. Saying the diuine office, or the office of our Bleſſed Lady, beſides all other Indulgences, they gaine 100. yeares of pardon.

7. Saying once euery day one *Pater Noſter* and *Aue Maria*, calling deuoutly three times vpon the Holy Name of Ieſus, they gaine

3000,

3000. yeares of Pardon.

8.   It is graunted vnto the Sisters that foure times a yeare they
may haue a generall absolution in
full remiffion of all their finnes
whatfoeuer, and be reftored to
the eftate of innocency, as fully as
they could receaue it from his Holines : & the like is graunted them
on euery feaft of our Bleffed Sauiour, our Bleffed Lady, on the feaft
of S. Peter and S. Paul, S. Fraci$,
S. Clare, S. Catharine Queene and
Martyr, the feaft of All Saints, and
euery day of the holy weeke ; yet
notwithftanding thefe graces will
profit nothing, vnto thofe who
fhould vpon prefumption to gaine
them, fin more freely. They may
apply all priuiledges and indulgences graunted to thēfelues, vnto
the

the faithfull departed. Note that
for the gayning of these or any indulgences is requisite the applying
of the intention for the same.

*An examen of Conscience for a Reli-
gious Person.*

VV H A T are his euill inclinations and bad cu-
stomes, whêce they pro-
ceed, & what warre & exercise he
vseth against them.

2. What Passions most raigne
in him, and by what meanes he
hath hitherto indeauoured to mor-
tify them.

3. What are his principall,
most frequent, and most trouble-
some temptations, and how he hath
hitherto behaued himself in them.

L 4   4. If

4.   If he be indifferent in accepting any imployment of the holy Religion, willingly accepting whatsoeuer is appointed him.

5.   Whether God be the only intention of all his actions, or if he seeke proper commodity or praise in his workes.

6.   Whether he doe not prefer exteriour matters, as good qualities and naturall gifts and graces, before the study of vertue and perfection.

7.   If he desire, and be most contented his Superiours should haue knowledge of all his faultes.

8.   If he be confident and open harted to his Superiours, & confer with them in any necessary occasion of things touching the good of his soule.

9.   Whe-

9 . Whether he be truly vnited by affection vnto his Superiors,
or if he haue any auersion, & from
whence it proceedes .

10 . Whether he be not too
familiar with some, and if that familiarity be not hurtfull to himself
and the other party , and if by that
occasiõ he loose not time, & disedi-
fy others .

11 . If he loue and imbrace the
interiour and exteriour mortifica-
tions, and rather those matters that
be hũble & abiect , then of esteeme
and credit .

12 . If he obserue al this Rules &
Constitutions, of which he maketh
lesse esteeme, & for what reason ,

13 . If he desire truly to be pe-
nitent for all his faultes ,truly con-
fessing them with strong purpose
of amendment.   L 5   14. If

14. If he make a particular examen euery day vpon one imperfection, and with what preparation he receaueth the holy Sacramēt: and how he frequenteth the holy exercise of prayer.

15. If his wordes & discourses in Recreation or otherwise, as also with secular be of edification: how he obserueth silence, and spendeth his time.

Twelue great Euills which come by Veniall sinnes.

FIRST, they doe so darken and obscure the eyes of our vnderstanding, that they cannot see almighty God. 2. They kill the feruour of dilection and diuine Charity. 3. They hinder our prayers
and

and petitions from being heard by
God. 4. They defile and spotte
the soule. 5. They contristate the
holy Ghost, and reioice the enemy.
6. They depriue vs of the sweet
and amiable familiarity of our Blessed Sauiour. 7. They are a great
cause and meanes of our fall into
more grieuous sinnes. 8. They
cause a soule to fall into great slouth
and tepidity in all goodnes. 9.
They weaké exceedingly the forces
of the soule, from resisting her
bad inclinations. 10. They incline
our affections and desires to temporall matters. 11. They prolong
and augment the paines in purgatory. 12. They exceedingly hinder vs from seeing & enioying the
presence of God.

Nyne

Nyne wayes by which we partici-
pate of the sinnes of others .

BY Counsell. 2. By commandment. 3. By consent 4. By pro-
curation or persuasion. 5. By
flattery. 6. By holding our peace of
his fault of whome we ought to
haue care. 7. To dissemble or not
to reprehend, and hinder if we be
thereunto obliged. 8. In participa-
ting of the matter, whereof such a
sinne doth proceed. 9. In defending
the fault of another .

Twelue fruits of the B. Sacrament.

IT not only maketh possible but
also most easy the forsaking and
leauing of all earthly & fading
thinges .   2. It

2. It causeth great profit & advancement in heauenly thinges.

3. It rayseth the soule aboue all things created.

4. It inforceth the spirit vnto all good.

5. It illuminateth and giueth light to the vnderstanding, in the knowledge of God.

6. It causeth an inflamed feruerous possession of the pure loue of God alone.

7. It is the consummation of al vertue & perfection.

8. It giueth the soule possession of the treasury of all goods & riches.

9. It causeth a continuall interiour ioy.

10. It indeweth her with a happy security & assurance, in seeing him

him in whome she belieueth.

11. A perfect peace beginning in this life & continuing for eternity.

12. A perfect vnió with almighty God, wherby the soule is made participant of all diuine perfection.

Twelue Euangelicall Counsayles.

POVERTY, wherby a Religious person is estranged from all terrestriall things.

2. Obedience without which no vertue is perfect.

3. Chastity which beautifieth and addorneth all other vertues.

4. Charity towardes our enemies, wherby all spirituall infection of any sinne is expelled.

5. Mansuetude, which (as sayth

S.

S. Ambrose) is the medicine of the hart, wherby the soule is illuminated by God Almighty, to knowne his secrets.

6. Mercy, which extendeth it selfe to the help of euery one without limite, entreth sweetly into the hart with pitty, & cleanseth it frō all sinne.

7. The simple word alwaies fructifying in God, in purity of intention, in charity &c.

8. Shunning occasion of sinne, conducting the soule with prudency, and security to the purchase of vertue.

9. Right intention, which maketh all workes to proceed of humility, to the edification of our neighbour.

10. Conformity of the worke

vnto

vnto the word, wherby all speciall inſtruction is ſeriouſly, & with all profit accepted.

11. Auoiding of vnprofitable ſolicitude, therby better to attend vnto ſpiritual illuminations, which are obſcured by earthly cares.

12. Fraternall Correction, which is a light that illuminateth the vnderſtāding, according to that of the Apoſtle, ſaying, That which is corrected is made apparent by the light that followeth.

The Malediction of S. Francis.

BY thee O Eternall, and Heauenly Father, and all the celeſtiall Court, and by me moſt Vnvvorthy, be accurſed all thoſe Brethren, vvho by their euill example doe ruine and deſtroy the thinges vvhich thou haſt built, and ceaſeſt not to build, by ſo many holy Brethren of this Order.

FINIS.